Don't Mute Moe

The Vision of an Urban Scholar

Don't Mute Moe

The Vision of an Urban Scholar

Ronald "Moe" Moten

with
Jeffrey Anderson

Dedications

My first dedication is to the loves of my life! My grandparents Thaddina and Edward Floyd who my family lost during the COVID pandemic. There would be no Moe without their unconditional love especially in times of need. They showed me that hard work and loving others are gifts from God. They embodied my favorite scripture Ecclesiastes 3:13 that says every man should eat, drink and work as if it's a gift from God! I work hard to accomplish every blessing I've received in life as I know their prayers continue to protect me and my family.

My second dedication is a special thanks to Al-Malik, founder of Cease Fire Don't Smoke the Brothers and Sisters. Upon my re-entry from prison in October 1994, Al-Malik opened the door to my activism and community organizing by making me the spokesperson for the organization and youth organizer for the Million Man March.

Moe's father Ronald Starks-El and Al-Malik
join him for his 50th birthday

Moe with his childhood friends
and their children at Cease Fire

Table of Contents

Acknowledgments

Ronald "Moe" Moten

I must start by thanking my creator, who allowed me to survive and overcome many mistakes, trials, and tribulations in my life—consistently endowing me with the power to translate the wisdom I gained from my journey to give back to those in my community, city, country, and the world who appreciate my work and have needed it the most.

Then there are my grandparents, Thaddinia and Edward Floyd to whom I have dedicated this book. I tragically and painfully lost both of them during the COVID pandemic in 2021 at a time when the healthcare system was overwhelmed. Their unconditional love, guidance, and wisdom still touch my heart and soul with every breath I take. I know my life would be different without their love, always providing a hand to pull me up just enough to get me back on my own two feet, knowing they had taught me all I needed to survive on my own.

Next, I want to thank my children for sharing me with the world. Thank you also to my parents Arlene Moten and Ronald Starks-El, loving souls who loved me unconditionally and were always there when I needed them. My father has been a role model for me in my transition to becoming a man, and he has advocated for me and treated my children as if they were his own. Even with all of their problems, they have been a blessing in disguise, teaching me that you can have flaws and still make great contributions to humanity. Their mistakes were sometimes the only reason I didn't fall victim to the pitfalls of drug addiction like many of my friends.

My first op-ed was published in the Outlook section of the *Washington Post* in 2006. I have a special place in my heart for former *Washington Post* editor and writer Dr. Natalie Hopkinson. She encouraged me to write my first op-ed and she featured me as a writer for the *Post* in several stories. We often talked about serious issues in our community. One day we were discussing a problem in our community, and she told me, "Moe, it's time for you to write on this issue." I was like, yes! I knew that I had a lot of wisdom in my head but had never put it on paper. I was a little intimidated, but when she said, "Don't worry, give it a shot, and I will edit it," the rest was history.

My first op-ed, "What's Snitching and What's Not," was written and published. It went viral worldwide as I received thousands of emails and the *Washington Post* comment section went wild. Our relationship continued and the fact that we did not always agree helped me sharpen my arguments and write better op-eds. I was a diamond in the rough, but we both had good intentions and many of the op-eds in this book are a result of the friendly friction between us.

I also would like to thank Jeffrey Anderson who I was once at war with over some of my ideas and activism. Now we have collaborated in publishing this book of my op-eds and Jeff's interviews with me about each one and their relevance to what is happening today. Jeffrey and other reporters and columnists like Nikita Stewart, Mike DeBonis, Courtland Milloy, Bruce Johnson, and Colbert King mostly wrote or broadcast positive stories about me, but I respect them because they were not afraid to honestly disagree with me. Evidence of our mutual respect is the fact that Colbert King wrote a very thoughtful endorsement for this book and Bruce Johnson wrote the foreword.

To this day Jeff and I don't entirely agree with each other, but that's fine because honest disagreement without animosity is what the world is missing today. I never ran from any reporter, and I was, and always will, be honest with them. I'm not perfect, but I don't lie, I don't steal, and I don't let people write things about me that are not true without fighting back. Because I did not run from his tough questions, Jeff and I got to know each other, and I am blessed that he agreed to partner with me on my second book. I am convinced that we have put together a timely and well-written book.

Then there are Jo-Ann Armao, Associate Editorial Page Editor and Jamie Riley, Letters and Local Opinions Editor, both from the *Washington Post*. These two women valued my opinion as a voice for my community, which meant a lot in my growth as a writer.

I would also like to thank Bruce Johnson, legendary news anchor, and Courtland Milloy, legendary *Washington Post* columnist, for always challenging and motivating me. They wrote or aired countless stories on my work, activities, opinions, and expertise. They might not know it, but they helped me understand why my work was so important and that was one of the main reasons why I didn't walk away from serving my people and the community during trying times.

I want to thank all the people who helped me behind the scenes when I was ambushed by D.C. politics and politicians. Deep thanks to people like Jimmy Kemp from the Jack Kemp Foundation, who helped fund my movement when all doors were closed, Scottie Irving and Sinclair Skinner, who were always a phone call away in a time of need. Many thanks to former Mayors Marion Barry, Anthony Williams, Adrian Fenty, and to current Mayor Muriel Bowser. Thank you also to Councilmembers Robert White, Kenyan McDuffie, and Brianne Nadeau, as well as former Councilmembers Kwame Brown and Jack Evans. These and other elected officials gave my movement funding and support even when my straight-shooting ways made others turn against me.

Karl Racine, D.C.'s first elected attorney general, is a man of his word and helped kill off false allegations, which had knocked me down to my knees and cost me everything I had. His actions set me up for my big comeback and to realize my purpose in life.

And to Douglas Jemal: Thank you for coming to the table and for supporting our cause.

Lastly, I want to thank Go-Go Music and D.C. Culture, the heartbeat of our city, which I've used to fight for change, educate, and motivate the people I've served for the last twenty-five years. The social power of music is something special. It is derived from the drum beat of our ancestors as they and we have been beaten up and down. That beat has always lifted the people up from Africa to D.C. Over the last 400 years, it's been the tool used by our ancestors and myself to stop the muting of the people and to ensure that no one could ever again mute our people or keep our fearless leaders from passing on to the next generation the beat of Go-Go and D.C. culture.

Finally, for my second set of eyes, my friend and publisher Curt Ashburn who looked over many of my op-eds before I sent them to various editors that published my work. This guy is just like Natalie. He saw something special in me when many didn't.

Acknowledgments

Jeffrey Anderson

When Ron Moten asked me to write this book with him, I was flattered, delighted, and worried that I didn't know what the hell I was doing. So I'd first like to thank Ron for inviting me to do something I had never done before, and for trusting me to help bring his hard-earned wisdom to these pages.

I'd also like to acknowledge my editors, colleagues, friends, sources, and fellow travelers of the past 25 years—a cast of characters who believed in me, inspired me, supported me, collaborated with me, argued with me, defended me, and tolerated me along the way.

As a reporter, I would not have come to the point of being involved with a project such as this without the comradeship of the following people:

Joe Donnelly, Katrina Dewey, Pearl Piatt, John Ryan, James Gordon Meek, Laurie Ochoa, Alan Mittelstaedt, Robert Greene, David Zahniser, Christine Pelisek, Van Smith, Ed Ericson, Jr., Chris Landers, Joe MacLeod, Matt Cella, David Lipscomb, Jerry Seper, Jim McElhatton, Chuck Neubauer, Tom Howell, Shaun Waterman, Allan Lengel, Colby King, Jamie Riley, Steve Cavendish and Andy DelGiudice.

Being a journalist isn't so much a job as it is a pursuit, a craft. You learn by doing it. Working with Ron on this book has given me an opportunity to undertake a different type of pursuit, and to begin learning a new craft. So I'd also like to thank our publisher, Curt Ashburn, and our copy editor, Braulio Agnese, two fine gentlemen whose knowledge, skill and experience have been invaluable.

And to my wife Kristin: My many thanks and undying love; I'd never be anywhere writing anything if it weren't for you.

Finally, I'd like to dedicate this to Max and his Pop.

About the Authors

Ronald Moten

Ronald "Moe" Moten is a fifth-generation Washingtonian educated in D.C. public schools where he attended Roosevelt Senior High School. He proudly hails from the now gentrified Petworth community where his grandparents raised him and instilled in him love for Washington, D.C. and for helping others. His trials and tribulations as a young man led him to serve time in Danbury and Allenwood Federal Correctional Institutions (FCI). While incarcerated, he obtained his GED and attended Park Community College where he majored in history and proudly mastered his knowledge of the Civil Rights Movement.

Choosing to formalize his education in African American and Native American history opened his mind and heart to the power of change and activism. Reading the works of great leaders such as Kwame Ture (Stokely Carmichael) and Winnie Mandela sparked a change in him. He committed himself to rebuilding his community. Upon his release from prison, he had a chance to meet and receive words of wisdom from leaders he had deeply admired but whom he had only read about. Moe became a student of the community, and the community embraced his thirst to make a positive difference.

Moe had the opportunity to study under great leaders such as Amelia Boynton Robinson, Dick Gregory, Pastor Gwendolyn Webb, Rev. Bone, Rev. James Orange, and Rev. James Bevel, who all served and advised Dr. Martin Luther King, Jr. Their words and actions showed Moe how to move proverbial mountains through faith and understanding that God works through fearless visionaries and their gifts to empower and uplift the community.

Immediately upon his release from Allenwood FCI, Moe began his work as the spokesperson and community organizer for Cease Fire Don't Smoke the Brothers and Sisters, a newly formed advocacy organization designed to ensure the protection of young Black children and adults. Granted a seat at the table with Mayor Marion Barry and Cease Fire founder Al-Malik, Moe and other young advocates from uptown D.C. and beyond were taught how and why to use the power of operating from the grassroots to the White House.

As a young man, he traveled around the country promoting and learning the science of peace. Moe is a natural innovator and skilled trainer in conflict resolution. He has helped broker more than forty truces between both male and female gangs in Washington, D.C. As co-founder and COO of Peaceoholics, Moe helped develop a structure that sent more than 160 at-risk youths to college. Many of those have returned home to become active in their communities as advisory neighborhood commissioners, lawyers, violence interrupters, and activists. He also assisted the city in developing numerous initiatives to combat violence. These include the Violence Intervention Partnership, Saving Our Sisters, and Rebuild the Village Model. During the time when Moe was involved in developing, operating, and training others in these programs, violent crimes in D.C. such as homicides decreased for four consecutive years after increasing for many years.

Moe and his staff helped train and hire over 360 returning citizens using the Peaceoholics model. Many of these men and women are now running their own organizations in D.C. following Moe's example. Moe and his co-workers came up with and promoted the use of the term

"Returned Citizen" to replace "ex-convict" and to give dignity to those who had been incarcerated. It is now used throughout the United States.

His first action in the trenches was in 1995 as a youth organizer for the Million Man March in Washington, D.C. He saw the miracle of a million African American men gathered non-violently to demand change and accountability.

While Black men and women were demanding to be heard in their cities, D.C. was fighting to keep its voice. The United States was in an uproar about the people of D.C. re-electing its beloved "Mayor for Life" Marion Barry. As a punishment, President Bill Clinton and Congress passed legislation that created the Control Board that had the power to override Barry and the D.C. Council on the city budget. The Control Board stripped D.C. schools of its trade and music programs, which was a path for many Washingtonians to the middle class. The city is still feeling the effects of that decision and the loss of the vocational programs has never been restored.

In an effort to address social, educational and economic disparities, Moe and leaders from Cease Fire Don't Smoke the Brothers and Sisters organized a massive youth protest. Children from DMV (the District, Maryland, Virginia metropolitan area) schools attended and the protest shut down the streets at Thomas Circle, a major thoroughfare in D.C. where the congressionally appointed Control Board had its headquarters. These two experiences exposed Moe to activism and insight on how legislation affects the people. From this point on, Moe would never be muted as he understood the power and purpose of his voice.

With over 25 years of experience, Moe continues to seek new avenues to support and empower his community. He is credited with transforming leaders of the local gay gang Check It. When it's leader Tayron Bennett reached out to Moe and asked him, "Why don't you ever help the gay children?" Moe told them, "We are all God's children, so if you are willing to help yourself, I'm eager to help you." The rest is history as many in the gang went from wreaking havoc and chaos in Gallery Place and around the DMV to being productive citizens.

Two of the leaders are majority partners of Check It Enterprises in Anacostia, a Southeast Washington, D.C. neighborhood. He has helped empower hard-working core leaders and founders of Check It to work with agencies and non-profits who provide services to at-risk LGBTQ youth and their peers. Moe helped Check It Enterprises expand and enhance its dream and business by serving as its life coach and connecting them to business mentors.

In 2016 Moten helped raise more than $70,000 in donations for renovating a property of Check It Enterprises including the "Secret Garden" and event space, which turned a blighted lot into a community hub. Moe has continued to help Check It with its vision and mission of becoming a community staple in Historic Anacostia and beyond. Together they purchased multiple properties after he convinced the D.C. government to step up and help them become the anchor for the preservation of D.C.'s culture in Moe's local and national fight against the negative effects of gentrification.

Moe is the co-founder of Don't Mute DC, which was sparked by the uproar against culture erasure by gentrifiers in D.C.'s Historic Shaw community. He and co-founder Dr. Natalie Hopkinson circulated a petition which collected over 80,000 signatures and became the grassroots spark that united D.C. and gave natives and other lovers of D.C.'s rich culture a much-needed victory at a time when many had given up and stopped fighting.

As this book goes to print, Moe and his partners at Check It Enterprises are opening the Go-Go Museum in Anacostia. He is also a proud member of the Kennedy Center's Culture Caucus and is launching the "Social Media Caucus" to address social media's adverse effects on youth and adults. He believes social media can be more of a positive tool to address many of the social ills and destructive behaviors that were magnified even more during the COVID pandemic.

Moe has learned from mentors and personal experiences that are exemplified by the words of Amelia Boynton Robinson, "When you hear voices or your intuition telling you what to do or write, listen because it's

God telling you what to do." At dinners in the Highlands Family Restaurant in D.C.'s Petworth neighborhood, the great Dick Gregory would tell him, "Boy shut up and listen. Don't waste my time." From that he learned that it is a blessing to listen and ask questions when a wise elder takes the time to share.

Being a leader requires a thick skin and always being ready to drink muddy water as he learned from a great Civil Rights Movement icon. Moe has learned to take the hate and envy with a grain of salt because all the BS ultimately helps your grass grow and your flowers bloom.

Ronald "Moe" Moten has received countless honors for his work including the McDonalds Community Leader Award, the 2020 Mayor's Arts Award for Community Advocacy, Search for Common Ground Award, Delta Sigma Theta Florence Letcher Toms Award for Outstanding Community Service, NAACP Outstanding Leadership Award in Juvenile Justice and was honored by the National Trial Lawyers Association.

Jeffrey Anderson

Photo credit: Andy DelGiudice

Jeffrey Anderson is an award-winning journalist and the editor of *District Dig*, D.C.'s premier source for longform journalism and investigative reporting on local government, politics and culture. His body of work spans from Los Angeles to Baltimore and Washington, D.C., and consists of in-depth reporting on criminal and civil justice, government corruption, and a wide range of social and political issues.

Jeff has probed monolithic institutions and local backwaters alike: The Catholic Church's clergy sex abuse scandal; Crime and corruption in the small, gang-ridden cities of Southeast L.A. County; Baltimore's "shadow" drug economy; and fraud, waste, and abuse in D.C. government.

He has earned numerous national and local awards for investigative reporting in his 25-year career, but it is his impact on public debate and government accountability that best defines his work.

Jeff's family is from Pawtucket, RI, and moved to Northern Virginia in 1970 when he was six-years-old. He played youth and varsity soccer and graduated from Annandale High School in 1982. He is a 1986 graduate of Colgate University where he majored in philosophy and played varsity soccer.

Anderson went to the law school then known as George Mason School of Law and worked part time as a law clerk. He graduated in 1991.

After practicing health law in Virginia and Los Angeles, he turned to writing and reporting in the late 1990s; first for *L.A. Daily Journal* and *LA Weekly*, then back east for *Baltimore City Paper*, the *Washington Times*, *Washington City Paper*, and *District Dig*, which he co-founded in 2016.

This is Jeff's first book writing project, and he hopes for more in the future.

Foreword

By Bruce Johnson

I don't remember when I first met Ron Moten. It's like I've always known him. He was always there when I arrived with my television crew after another horrendous shooting in the hood. Whether it was a college student coming back home for summer break, a young man who dropped out of school with no parent or truant officer to come looking for him, or the kid who demonstrated promise in the classroom or on the athletic field, the bullets flying through our Black communities didn't care where they landed or who was taken out.

Ron Moten was built to make a difference in these areas. He knew what the city leaders could only guess! By age 21 he had been part of the violence and the crack epidemic. After escaping death in a car chase with bullets flying at him, Moten ended up in prison. He had no excuses.

The product of a working-class family raised in a middle-income neighborhood in Petworth, God's grace must have touched Moe while incarcerated and told him there was a heart and talent inside him that could be put to much better use. In 2004, he founded an organization to save young lives. He recruited formerly incarcerated individuals and local Go-Go performers and paid them decent salaries when they succeeded in bringing peace and quiet to once violent neighborhood crews.

I didn't appreciate the name "Peaceoholics" when I first heard it. I really thought it a bad idea when Moten and his partner Jauhar Abraham would yell at city council members in public forums about the youth violence.

I came to understand that shouting is what was needed at the time. People, including young victims were dying in the streets. There would have been hell to pay if the same violence was killing people who looked different or lived in different more affluent neighborhoods.

Ron Moten was persuasive! We talked nearly every day and night and most weekends. How do we stop the gunplay, the hurt, the loss of another generation? His enthusiasm and perseverance won me over as a reporter and eventually a friend. Moe is a man of his word.

I still marvel at how he convinced former Mayors Anthony Williams and Adrian Fenty to give Peaceoholics millions of dollars to fund their programs. It was, in my opinion, money well spent, although a former Attorney General and some city politicians thought otherwise.

Moe was forced to move away from his nonprofit anti-violence efforts for a while, but a subsequent AG and Mayor urged him back to the front lines as the violence surged yet again.

Civil rights icon Andrew Young, a lieutenant for Dr. Martin Luther King, Jr. once told me that "none of us in the civil and human rights movement retired with a pension." Moe has made a similar sacrifice!

He's given most of his adult life to an anti-violence movement that brings no financial reward. There won't be a pension.

No other voice in the District of Columbia carries the same authenticity when it comes to our young people who face the kinds of decisions that most other youth can defer.

There are hundreds if not thousands of kids who not only survived the streets because of Ron Moten, they are now thriving because of Moe!

Tragically, on April 3, 2022, as this book was about to go to the printer, Bruce Johnson died of heart failure. He was 71. Mr. Johnson devoted 44 years of his remarkable career as an anchor, reporter, and author, to telling groundbreaking stories for WUSA9 in a signature style that endeared him to Washingtonians. Called "a giant in broadcast journalism" by his peers, his work has been recognized with 22 Emmys, the Edward R. Murrow Award, and induction into the Society of Professional Journalists Hall of Fame. Mr. Johnson was the founder of the Bruce Johnson Group. At the time of his passing, he had been devoting his time to writing, lecturing, and public speaking. His second book, Surviving Deep Waters, *was published in February 2022.*

Introduction

R on Moten and I were sitting on a picnic bench in Anacostia Park, Southeast Washington, D.C., near the Pirate Ship Playground on a windy day in March 2020, doing what we thought would be the final interview for this book. Children were climbing all over the ship, and a few seniors were doing old-school calisthenics nearby.

Just behind us, within earshot, a group of four or five young men were gathered at a table underneath a gazebo—guys in their late teens and early 20s, chopping it up by the side of the river that separates their community from the rest of the city. Their conversation sounded intense; at times, voices were raised. Though I couldn't make out precisely what they were saying, there wasn't any of the laughter you ordinarily hear when dudes are hanging out and talking trash.

Of course, there's not much to laugh about if you are a young Black man in the District of Columbia. With racial disparity and gentrification have come alienation and displacement; with poverty and loss have come violence, more violence, and, yes, anger. That last and most dangerous of emotions could be projected onto various demographics and circumstances, yet it also has turned inward, to an alarming degree. The generation that is now coming of age—in between the little ones playing and the old-timers exercising in this beautiful park—is killing itself, day by fatal day.

Suddenly, Moe—as most people call the renowned activist-turned-entrepreneur—makes eye contact with one of the young men and offers his customary greeting: "What's up, soldier? You good?"

> Moe's words are not intended to tell you what you want to hear. He's going to tell you what he thinks you need to hear, to encourage you to chart your own course, and to inspire you to take control of your own destiny.

1

The young man, tall and thin, ambles over, one foot in a walking boot. "You know you saved me, man. My friend, he's got a record on him now, but you helped me when I needed it. I'm straight. I wouldn't lie to you."

There's no way to confirm if this is true, that's not the point. He's showing respect, bringing a smile to Moten's face, a trace of gratification, if not pride. Here is another young person in this city whose life he has touched in the name of violence reduction, community development, and personal growth. He confesses he doesn't even know this guy's name.

"There's many of them," I remind him, "but one of you."

Tragically, about a mile away and at roughly the same time, just over the Frederick Douglass Bridge near Nationals Park, two girls, aged 13 and 15, are tasing a Pakistani UberEats driver in a botched carjacking that leaves the 66-year-old immigrant, husband, father and grandfather dead on the ground.

Biking home after we wrap the interview, I pass an EMS unit headed to what we soon learn is a deadly scene. I call Ron—out of habit I still call him by his first name—and we are struck by this chilling parallel. Why? Because the dysfunction in the lives of these young 'uns—to borrow a frequent expression in Moten's vocabulary—is central to a dialogue we'd been having less than an hour before, and for the last three years since we started this book project.

Actually, it's a dialogue we've been having for more than a decade.

I first encountered Moten in 2009, at the scene of a shooting in Congress Heights. I was writing a freelance article on his former violence interruption outfit Peaceoholics, a group that positively affected many lives, yet became mired in controversy over cronyism and city funding. My 6,000-word exposé for Washington *City Paper* contributed to the negative scrutiny. Ron was not pleased, and he let me (and the editor) know about it. It's a memory we often laugh about.

We talked about the shortcomings of politicians and government officials—in particular, officials at the Department of Youth Rehabilitation Services, back then a mismanaged agency that is largely overlooked to this day for the role it has played in the lives of thousands of D.C. youths. We talked about the struggles of those children, the lack of guidance in the home, the lack of positive role models in the community, the lack of opportunity in society. We realized during these discussions that we were looking through our respective lenses—mine, as that of a journalist; Ron's, as that of an activist and community advocate—and seeing the same picture.

When I occasionally comment on Ron's choice to set aside a "beef" with a reporter and opt for what has become a lasting relationship built on mutual respect and trust, he just shrugs and says, "That's what men do."

Just about anyone is capable of carrying a grudge, and he and I are no different. But the fact is, if more teenagers, young men and women, and full-grown adults were able and willing to set aside differences, affronts, perceived slights, or signs of disrespect instead of going to the gun so early, so often, then maybe there'd be more hope and less trauma in the Black D.C. community.

To cynical observers, holding out such hope might sound idealistic, myopic, or naive. Ron does not do cynicism, though. He's always moving forward. Once, if someone posed a threat to him, his community, or his interests—it could be a complaint over loud Go-Go music blaring from a storefront, lack of support for a hospital or halfway house, a land grab that messed with his development plans—he'd "go to war" by publicly berating his opponent. These days, he's more likely to handle his business in a low-key manner, one that gets results without the hard feelings that come from overt criticism.

It's that pivot from loud, in-your-face street fighter to self-possessed facilitator that has allowed him to realize dreams larger than the ones he had when we first met. Such as "Don't Mute DC," a movement-turned-project that has:

- made Go-Go the official music of Washington, D.C.
- launched an oral history in collaboration with the Smithsonian Center for Folklife and Culture
- restored funding for United Medical Center and Banneker Academic High School

- rescued funding for Project Empowerment's work with returned citizens and at-risk populations
- become a member of the Culture Caucus at the Kennedy Center.

Ron has learned that, just as a beef need not end with a body in the morgue, a business or political conflict need not turn into a spectacle.

His evolved brand of citizenship, activism, entrepreneurial drive, and sense of purpose has come from the opposite of counterproductive impulses. It has come from faith. Faith in himself. Faith in God. Faith in young people—who, he believes, are capable of rising above society's assumptions that tell them they have no value and no chance, and therefore nothing to lose in taking another's life, even at their own expense.

In our society, it seems as if jail too often means too little to a kid without a father, with a father who is in jail, or with a father who is physically (or mentally or emotionally) abusive. Carjacking for profit or for kicks and bragging about it on social media does not seem to come with fear or dread of death or a felony murder conviction.

Ron has been wrestling with these issues for years. The path has been rocky—sometimes of his own making. But a prison stint for drug dealing in the 1990s, he says, saved him. Bad press hardened him. Peace activism and the study of civil rights history redeemed him.

He has his detractors, but it's hard to deny the impact Ron has had in his community. His industriousness has earned him respect among city leaders, who in 2020 approved a grant that funded the purchase of the storefront home of Check It Enterprises, a community hub he co-founded with former gang members that is a business incubator, future site of D.C.'s first Go-Go Museum, and home to the multi-use, cultural, and spiritual destination known as "The Secret Garden."

Along the way, he has published more than a dozen op-eds, in the *Washington Post*, the *Washington Times*, the *Washington Informer*, and on my website, *District Dig*. Those writings examine the present in terms of a past that has foretold the future. And they speak to what's at stake if history continues to repeat itself.

So: Why should you dive into this collection of Moten's often stern-sounding op-eds, his common-sense lectures, and his cautionary musings on topics as diverse as policing, social media, charity, and snitching?

First, Moe—that's short for "Moten" and it's the name he's known by in the community—is a great speaker and his words translate well into writing. Moe's words have clarity and purpose. Second, you can't mute Moe, thus the title of the book. He has been knocked down many times, but he always comes back. He lives by and acts on the principles he writes about in these op-eds. Moe knows—and I know this from being a journalist—that you learn by doing, and that by doing, you motivate others to pursue their talents.

It was three years ago now that we began a series of interviews to introduce these published pieces, we both wanted to motivate others to not only write down their thoughts, stories, and opinions, as he has, but to act and demonstrate the "power of the pen." We also wanted to document his journey as a returned citizen, anti-violence activist, youth mentor, historian, and author, as well as an advocate for economic inclusion. We wanted to show how topics he addressed years ago—such as how violence and criminality depicted in computer games, simulations, and interactive videos are corroding idle minds and inciting dangerous tendencies in youth—ring as true today as when he first wrote about them.

We also hoped to spark a dialogue about the values he both espouses and embodies, such as self-empowerment, self-direction, and taking responsibility. Moe's words are not intended to tell you what you want to hear. He's going to tell you what he thinks you need to hear, to encourage you to chart your own course, and to inspire you to take control of your own destiny. He has seen firsthand the power of positivity. He has lived it, and he preaches it.

Finding a way to achieve personal and community goals, he says, positions people to show others a way forward. It reminds them to never let their voices be muted.

And that, Moe knows, is no laughing matter, either.

—Jeffrey Anderson

Chapter 1

Grand Theft Morals

Moe and I sat down for our first interview on August 6, 2019, in the basement of Check It Enterprises on Martin Luther King Jr. Avenue in downtown Anacostia, across from the Big Chair. Until the pandemic arrived, we did all our interviews here, sitting across from each other on metal chairs, our voices echoing off concrete, white-painted walls in the large, empty space—an enlarged photograph of legendary jazz poet- musician Gil Scott-Heron looking down on us.

He chose this *Washington Post* op-ed for the first chapter in light of persistent increases in homicides and carjackings, a proliferation of hyperviolent video games, and the use of social media as a forum for boasts and glorification of crime and gangsterism, both virtual and real. It amazed me that Moe had written about this back in 2012, and that his revelation dated back even further, to 2005, when he visited the Department of Youth Rehabilitation Services' infamous Oak Hills Youth Center and found a group of kids playing *Grand Theft Auto*. As a violence interrupter, youth counselor and mentor with Peaceoholics, he was disturbed to see this.

"Some of them were locked up for stealing cars and robbing people," he said. "You just know these [videos] have an influence. When I looked at children who might come from single parent households or pockets of violence, I knew it was gonna have to have an effect on them. Like when

6

you saw the Columbine shooting, those guys played violent video games that taught them how to kill. You knew they'd be desensitized to heinous behavior like that. So it was not rocket science to predict things were gonna get worse. I mean, they use these same games to train our military professionals and people who protect our country on how to fight in war. So if they used this to train people to fight in war, why wouldn't we see that it will be used to train our children to be terrorists within our own community?"

Moe told me he recently found *Grand Theft Auto* on a computer in his own home, and he was furious. Newer, even more violent games are coming onto the market all the time, he said of a gaming industry that experts project to generate more than $200 billion by 2023. "A lot of them are people killing people. A lot of them show people robbing people. People carjacking people, people using drugs … we've had hundreds of real opioid deaths so far in 2021. They glorify drugs and violence. They use slang from the games. I mean, these are the things that we're seeing now, and it's been accepted as part of our culture now."

I asked him if states regulated the sale of these games, and he said he and others had protested Rockstar Games in 2005 and pushed for legislation to keep such products out of the hands of young people. Hillary Clinton took a public stand, but Moe felt she capitulated to industry pressure and threats of First Amendment legal challenges. "I'll never forget," he said. "Hillary Clinton had spoken after one of our big protests in New York, and it was in the *New York Post*, and she spoke against the video games, and a month later she was at the Hilton Hotel speaking at their conference."

Faced with corporate resistance to regulation, ineffective government intervention, and lack of parental supervision in his community, Moe is concerned about at-risk children being left on their own to separate virtual gaming from reality. Some studies have shown that games like *Grand Theft Auto*, when played repeatedly, can contribute to an increase in aggressive behavior, as well as decreases in positive social behavior, sensitization to violence, and empathy. Causation between playing video games and the real thing is hard to quantify, but homicides have surged in recent years, and carjackings are rampant.

"I think most young people have been brainwashed because of lack of opportunities, lack of resources, and low self-esteem, that the most powerful person and popular person on the block is the one with the biggest gun," Moe said. "Everybody wants to be the coolest person on the block. Young people will try to emulate what they see. Some people are lonely, want to make a name for themselves. Some people feel like they want to inflict pain upon other people. And some people have peer pressure."

Even adults are into violent video games, he noted. "They play them just as much as children! A lot of them play—no question about that."

As we talked, it seemed he had become disheartened by the lack of data on the various causes of violence that can be linked to visual entertainment and video games. He said he thinks they go hand-in-hand with drugs. "I don't think nobody wants to hear the truth. But like I said, we know the young person without guidance, playing violent video games, smoking weed, and popping mollies—you can see a gradual elevation to negativity with people doing these things."

Moe has urged D.C. Council members to bring back legislation to ensure that parents and merchants are obligated to keep certain games "out of the hands and minds of our children." That was a decade ago, and yet we're still having the same conversation.

"Have you given up on that initiative? I asked.

"I might bring it back up. I mean, you gotta have legislators who will really go against a powerful industry. They don't care about our children dying. They care about the dollars. Some people got a moral conscience, some people don't. There was a time in America when certain things wouldn't make it to the TV set or get on the radio. Now every other video, video game, or song refers to those things."

Violence on the Screen, Violence in the Streets

Washington Post, December 28, 2012

By Ron Moten

It was 2005, but I remember it like it was yesterday. Jauhar Abraham, who co-founded Peaceoholics with me, and I were headed to Oak Hill Youth juvenile detention facility to conduct group sessions with troubled youths. When we walked into the facility, we found the teenagers glued to the TV playing "Grand Theft Auto," a video game in which players steal cars and otherwise commit murder and mayhem in huge amounts. Many of these youths wound up where they were for committing crimes very like the ones they were committing in the video game. Needless to say, we were outraged.

To find out what kind of impact such games had on them, we held focus groups with the youths. I recall one of them telling me that, before he started playing the games, he would have never gotten into a stolen car, a step which led to stealing cars later on and eventually to violent carjackings—just like in the game. Then one youth I will never forget said that playing the games put him "in a zone" to do what he had to do to survive. This young man would later be killed, and after his death several murders would be attributed to him.

It was obvious that the violent games desensitized these youths to violence. But I didn't really need them to tell me this. The focus groups brought back memories of when I was growing up. I was just as easily influenced by the entertainment industry. Many of my friends either wanted to be like Michael Jordan—or Scarface.

Did we idolize Jordan because he was the most exciting basketball player of all time? Or could it have been because he showed up in pretty much every other commercial on television? Scarface was a different story. Tony Montana—Al Pacino's character in the movie of that name—was admired for how he rose in the drug game. I saw the influence firsthand when some of my friends began saying, "Say hello to my little friend"—

Montana's famous line—before committing acts of violence similar to what they saw glorified in the film.

Abraham and I knew we had to do something with what we were learning about the negative impact of violent media. With the support of civil rights activists, we set out to train youths who were once members of rival gangs to become activists. During our sessions with them, we discussed the impact of violent video games. They came to see themselves as change agents with the power to stop this poison from reaching their peers.

We had some successes with our work and started attracting media attention. Adrian Fenty and Jim Graham took the lead on D.C. Council legislation aimed at stopping violent and sexually explicit games from getting into the hands of minors. But once the powerful lobbyists from the video game industry got involved, it all went nowhere.

Now we have seen the horrific massacre in Newtown, Conn., and we're having the same conversation all over again. For District residents, the violence displayed in Newtown is all too familiar. In 2010, five young people were killed and nine wounded in the South Capitol Street massacre, only a few miles from where our president resides. Data show that murder is down in the District, but this is misleading to some degree. Since 2005, thousands have fallen victim to assaults, stab wounds and gunshots—all of which our children act out daily in video games that grow more violent all the time.

And yet some continue to argue that our violence-infested entertainment cannot possibly influence an individual to commit acts of terror. They are wrong.

It's time for the District's legislators to bring back the bill ensuring that parents and merchants are obligated to keep these games out of the hands—and minds—of our children. Additionally, we must ensure that every child in America who needs mental health services gets them while also stopping them from self-medicating through violent games. Remember, hurt people hurt people. Let's all be responsible and act before the next massacre.

Chapter 2

Give Them a Stage or They Will Create One

Roughly a decade after he wrote in the *Washington Post* about the effects of violent video games, Moe did this piece for my website, *District Dig*. I had been wanting him to write for me for some time.

Due to the pandemic, we are sitting down in Anacostia Park, near the Pirate Ship. I think he chose this piece for the second chapter because it highlights the flipside of the influences about which he wrote in the first chapter: platforms for communication and expression. Except that, in this case, he was reacting to a recent attempt by the city to legislate the volume of live music and public performances, modes of expression that he'd like to see more of.

> If we don't figure out a way to make it fun for people to get attention in the right way, then this destructive behavior is going to incriminate a lot of young people for the rest of their lives.

I had just run across The Experience Band out on 14th Street in Northwest on a sunny day. They had raised my spirits. Very funky, and very D.C. Go-Go at its most primal—just buckets and drumsticks—is great. Throw some horns and other instruments into the mix, and it goes to a whole new level.

While many understand Go-Go to be a joyous sound and an uplifting, original D.C. art form, Moe also sees it—and music in general—as a platform that can be a positive influence for young people whose lives are full of challenges to overcome, risks and traps to avoid. Isolation during the pandemic has only heightened the contrast between that and the corrosive effects of violence in the media and gaming industry. "The pandemic has affected a lot of things I've done over the past years that create the opportunity for people to come together and talk and bond and address issues. So, you know, that human-to-human connection has been kind of taken away. And you can't really touch or even hold people accountable the same way as you do in person."

Though COVID has shown us the value of digital tools that keep us connected, people surrounded with negativity are missing outlets that offer a more positive path, says Moe. "Now, a lot of young people, whether they were football players, boxers, dancers, models, student leaders—those things were eliminated in many communities even before COVID. A lot of young people I work with, they don't have the opportunity to escape what I call hell on earth and make the best of it."

So they turn to virtual media? "There are all types of forms of media for good and bad," he says, citing disturbing Instagram posts by youths whose crimes are being documented in real time on Twitter by an emerging brand of citizen journalists who monitor police scanners.

Not long ago, Moe had told me about these social media platforms on which young people are boasting of their crimes, recreating them, or actually filming them, which I found both shocking and kind of dumb. "So now we have a situation where a lot of our young people are getting attention through various forms of media that are homegrown, urban-created, and they thrive off of getting attention by any means necessary," he says. "If we don't figure out a way to make it fun for people to get attention in the right way, then this destructive behavior is going to incriminate a lot of young people for the rest of their lives."

I tell him I still can't figure out why they would do this.

"One: I think a lot of young people feel like they don't have nothin' to lose," Moe explains. "So they're not thinking about the consequences of what they're doing. Two: In some cases, they've been taught that there are no consequences." For many, he says, the wakeup call comes too late—and when it does, no one is paying attention anymore. The juvenile justice system, if it fails to rehabilitate youth offenders, once they are no longer spared adult punishment, they become forgotten.

In fact, the D.C. Council is currently looking at more ways to shield youths from the adult criminal justice system—unless, Moe notes, a White person or tourist gets killed. Yet even if they stay out of prison, the clock is still ticking for them to turn their lives around. The potential consequences are daunting, for the youth and for an overburdened mass incarceration system that is not the answer: "Now you're 18 years old, looking at 20, 30 years. "You've been used to getting away with stuff. Now nobody is going to take it lightly. Nobody cares about you once you become an adult."

Go-Go has saved more than one D.C. native from such a fate. Moe had a press conference in February 2021 to announce the resolution of a property dispute with mega-developer Douglas Jemal over the outdoor space behind the Check It Enterprises storefront known as "The Secret Garden." (More on that in Chapter 16: What a Crane Will Never Lift.) Backyard Band leader and one of the co-stars on the popular HBO series The Wire, Anwan "Big G" Glover, spoke about how Go-Go got him off the street, and probably saved his life.

Not everyone can get as famous as Backyard, though. Just as not everyone can become a star by rapping in a positive manner, Moe says, referring to two prominent recording artists, Common and J. Cole.

Besides, what's better than becoming a binding force in your own community, he asks—a force for good. "Well, street performers, they benefit from it in more ways than one. When you help people heal, it helps you heal and helps you grow. Everybody knows this music is magical to people. If you walk past and the Future Band or The Experience Band is playing, it makes you feel good, and that makes them feel inspired, and motivated. You see different people who normally don't come together come together loving what they see, in peace together, and it's something the world is missing today."

There are even more practical concerns to keeping Go-Go alive, he says, in the clubs and in the streets. "A lot of these people make money off of this, and they'll tell you, 'Look if I didn't start doing this, my thing was robbing people.' With Go-Go music, it heals the soul. These are the things that made D.C. exciting, gave it our culture, gave the less fortunate an option. You want to ask, 'Why would you discourage this or try to mute it?'"

Experience Band starred as street performers on U Street. Its leader was once homeless. Music was his springboard.

Eliminating Another Positive Platform During COVID Will Lead to More Violence in the Community

District Dig, March 8, 2021

By Ron Moten

Today I received several emails about the D.C. Council reintroducing a bill to basically mute D.C. street performers. For the third time since 2018, city officials are threatening to outlaw street performances above a certain volume, and to fine violators up to $300.

This feeds right into an op-ed I planned to write explaining reality to city leaders who don't understand the consequences of social and racial disparities, cultural erasure and a lack of positive platforms for young people to give expressive coloration to their inner conflicts and dreams.

What these leaders often see as inexplicable violence, is exacerbated by their own insistence on silencing the voices of our young people. Though we have always had spikes in violence, I can tell you that in my 25 years of addressing street violence, this current one is a different monster with many root causes.

But I can also tell you that some of those causes can be avoided.

Even growing up in D.C. during the crack epidemic, young people had numerous positive activity outlets and platforms to get attention and advance their God-given talents. Then, as now, those talents not only included a broad range of sports, but also things like dancing and teen Go-Gos, or even joining Go-Go bands, marching bands, modeling teams, chess clubs, debate teams, talent shows, hair shows, choirs and other opportunities to hustle legally to make money to buy things that appealed to us that many of our parents couldn't afford.

Many Washingtonians remember Junkyard Band and Backyard Band started their careers playing on buckets in Georgetown and other areas of D.C. Talk to them now, and they will tell you that this was the difference between them and many of their friends they lost to the streets of D.C.

Sadly, many of those activities and platforms that existed for generations of Washingtonians have systematically evaporated over the last

25 years, contributing to the nightmare of violence we are living through today.

The Internet and social media have become platforms where many young people seek attention. But far too many get attention using these platforms to glorify or participate in acts that hurt their communities and ruin their futures. We see their brief fascination with thousands of likes on urban social media handles such as @DMVHOODZNEWS and @MurderMayhem. We watch them incriminate themselves with senseless acts of violence, often blatantly brandishing guns in places like the Anacostia Metro, where they know countless cameras are recording them.

Yet they still are willing to pull the trigger.

They talk about their crimes both before and after they commit them, just for the attention they get by people rooting them on and encouraging them on these very same platforms.

Today, many of our youths could care less about the consequences of their actions, because many are living for the moment and feel as if they do not have a future. Not long ago, we would be rooting for the same child to hit the game-winning jump shot, applauding them as they mimic a Michael Jackson dance, or praising them for winning the spelling bee or D.C. science fair—as I once did as a child. (It was, and still is, one of the best feelings I ever experienced.)

It's the job of community leaders, families and city government to give our young people more positive platforms like the very one they are trying to eliminate with this new bill. Look at the opportunity that "Malik the Dope Drummer" got from the confidence and artistic development of being a street performer. He is now internationally known and is representing our city, making it to the finals on the hit TV show "America's Got Talent."

Another example is The Experience Band, which also is headed to stardom, as they bring joy to diverse crowds on Historic U Street on any given night.

Contrast such positivity with the rash of carjackings here in D.C. and nationwide, and it becomes clear that elected leaders have to decide whether they want to encourage young people to pursue their talents out in the community or leave them to seek attention on social media by committing senseless acts of violence while live streaming their destructive behavior as their own real-time versions of a Grand Theft Auto chase.

I see weekly now where Prince George's County Police are chasing young people in cars either stolen or carjacked, speeding into D.C. and zooming right past my house.

History calls for our city leaders to be creative and help provide more responsible ways to open more doors—not less—and to give our young people platforms to use their talents the right way. We are still waiting for them to create a track or league for four-wheelers, just as we created skateboard parks for skateboarders who once were an issue for some.

We must expand opportunities for our young people to get the attention they seek and to express themselves, rather than eliminate or suppress outlets for them to develop their talents and work out their inner conflicts.

Understand this: These young people, like every other generation, will find ways to get our attention. Nobody—neither you, nor me, nor the city council—is immune from the violent consequences of muting D.C.

Chapter 3

Forgotten Identity

I'm not gonna lie: When Moe was talking about college kids, a campus fence, and a historic cemetery in the same sentence, in this 2013 *Washington Times* op-ed, I was not sure where he was going.

He was struck by the sight of students jumping the fence of Howard University's annual homecoming celebration to catch the entertainment acts, after so few had answered Congresswoman Eleanor Holmes Norton's call for a day of community service for the revival of Woodlawn Memorial Cemetery, where so much Black history is buried. Does that sound like a reach? Not for Moe.

When I first met him, in 2009, he was facing a political backlash related to Peaceoholics and his close relationship with then-Mayor Adrian Fenty. After the controversy died down, he took time to reflect and study. Having taken college courses in prison, he already was fluent in civil rights history

> Young people don't know where they come from. And that's one of the biggest travesties for the African American community. Lotta people are afraid to say that's a problem. But that's a big problem.

and had met and been inspired by civil rights leaders and foot soldiers in the movement such as Gwendolyn Webb, Kwame Ture, Amelia Boynton Robinson, and James Bevel, all of whom had worked with Dr. Martin Luther King Jr.

He wanted to revisit those grassroots lessons and pass them on, so he began taking Black youths down the U.S. Civil Rights Trail in the Deep South. (Moe also published his first book, *Drinking Muddy Water*, became a Republican for a time, and ran for D.C. Council, kicking his campaign off at the hallowed Woodland Cemetery where John Mercer Langston, founder of Howard University Law School, is buried.)

"I did a lot of research and saw all these civil rights icons who were buried there," he tells me, in the fall of 2019, in the basement of Check It Enterprises. "Some of them went to Howard, and I have two grandparents that are buried there too. And I found all that out, and I'm like: Look at these damn people jumping over a fence for a show, but none of them are going to Woodlawn asking, 'How do I fix this cemetery of Black excellence? How do I learn about the history of these great people here and use that to better my life, my community, and learn from what they did and also honor what they did?'"

Moe hews to a strong line where curiosity and regard for Black history is concerned among young people—who, by comparison, know all the words to all the hottest rap songs. He ventures that most Howard students don't know half of what lies in the cemetery in Benning Ridge, a short distance—but a world away—from their privileged campus.

"So one of the biggest problems of African Americans is two things," says Moe, using one of his classic turns of phrase: "Either we neglect, don't embrace, or are not aware of our history—or our history is destroyed. And when you look at other races, other groups, most of them know their history, where they came from, and it's passed on to their children, which gives them a sense of pride, determination, and respect for their elders or OGs. These issues were very important to me because I was aware of the sacrifices people made for us to be in the position we are in. You can't not know this history and call yourself Black, or a leader in the Black community. Because we have a loss of what values are real values, we out here jumping over a fence instead of taking care of our ancestors' graves and their history and things that mean something."

Moe says adults in the community owe it to future generations to learn and respect this history and pass on their wisdom and understanding of the suffering and sacrifice of the leaders of the civil rights movement. "Like, young people don't know where they come from. And that's one of the biggest travesties for the African American community. Lotta people are afraid to say that's a problem. But that's a big problem."

Why is there such a gap?

"Well, it's a couple of things. One: the school system doesn't teach it. Two: a lot of people in our community don't know their history for decades. And three: we don't make it attractive to the youth. One of the biggest things that we did with Peaceoholics is we made it cool not to be a fool. You have to make it cool for people to learn."

When mentors from the group were overseeing in-school suspensions at Ballou Senior High School, he says, they would challenge kids to take their ancestors' sacrifices and their education more seriously than their pop culture icons and their own rivalries and beefs. "People died for our freedoms, and you come to school and be in a damn fight," he says.

One of the things that holds his community back, Moe says, is low expectations, from outside and from within. It's a matter of personal responsibility, and accountability, to be informed, he says, revealing the conservative roots that caused him to leave the Democratic Party and become a "Civil Rights Republican" in the image of Abraham Lincoln. (He has since left the GOP and become an Independent.) And he's not talking about being fluent in the history of Biggie and Tupac. "Why would I want to be around people who don't want to know their history? You don't want them to know how much power they have. You don't want them to know what people before them did."

Take Langston, a civil rights pioneer who founded Howard's law school and was interim president of the university. "That's huge," Moe says. "These people, man, you look at the time they were living in, they did some things that were inconceivable during a time where it's like, you've been fighting against Hell and to see them do this, it gives you power for all you go through."

He's referring to icons like Nannie Helen Burroughs, who had a school in D.C. where she taught Black people how to embrace their history through education, determination, economics, and purpose; and to Booker T. Washington, who once visited Burroughs here in the nation's capital.

"All of these great leaders who were fighters, they made sure that we knew our history, that we knew what we could do, that we could shoot for excellence instead of jumping over a damn fence. So when you look at these types of people, it makes it so that you never give up."

Reviving Howard University Could Start With Reviving Woodlawn's History

Washington Times, October 30, 2013

By Ron Moten

Observing black youth participating in a chaotic scene jumping the fence of Howard University's annual homecoming celebration was hard to stomach. Apparently, getting to see the concert that included national music artists was worth both the dangers of scaling the fence and violent encounters with the police. It is sad to think that few if any of these students responded to last week's call by Congresswoman Eleanor Holmes Norton to turn out and help lead the revival of the historic Woodlawn Cemetery where a wealth of black history is buried. The men and women interred inside the fence of Woodlawn did much more for the current generation of black Americans than any of the well-known, but hardly historic, entertainers performing inside the fence at Howard University.

The historic figures buried in that obscure cemetery helped to simultaneously uplift America and a race of people both figuratively bound by the legacy of slavery. One well-marked grave is that of John Mercer Langston (1829-1897), the first black man elected to public office in U.S. History. Langston was not only the great-uncle of the famous poet Langston Hughes, but also the first appointed president of Howard University and the dean of the law school, which he helped found. In 1889 he became the first black Civil Rights Republican elected to congress in the state of Virginia.

The vast majority of the young leaders lost their composure when told Rap artist "2 Chainz" was just slated to perform. The up-and-coming leaders could recount plenty of stories about multi-talented millionaire celebrity Howard alumnus Sean "Puff Daddy" Combs, but none of the students interviewed knew the name John Mercer Langston. Another great Civil Rights Republican buried at Woodlawn is Blanche Kelso Bruce

(1841-1897) who served Mississippi as the second elected black U.S. Senator and the first to serve a full term.

One of the most important lessons of history is that if we as black Americans do not tell our story to the next generation, other people will tell our story for us. A race that does not control the content of its own history dooms the generations to follow. Holmes Norton's invitation was an opportunity for Howard students to make the historic Woodlawn Memorial Cemetery part of their homecoming week by adding a little known, but proud spirit of freedom to their homecoming celebration. Norton did her best to use her own place in history to bring attention to a place where great businessmen, surgeons, church founders and many Howard alumni are memorialized.

How many Howard students know about prominent female attorney Clara Burrill Bruce (1882-1947) who was married to the son of Blanche Bruce and was the second black woman to pass the Massachusetts State bar examination? Then there is Lillian Evanti who graduated from Howard University with a bachelor's degree in music who is famous for being the first black American female opera singer and toured throughout Europe and South America. Both of these barrier-breaking women were proudly laid to rest at Woodlawn.

The passing on of these names and their legacies to the current generation has been neglected. There is no wonder why so many of our youth are lost. In recognition of these great Civil Rights Republicans, my campaign for the Ward 7 City Council seat was kicked off at Woodlawn Cemetery. This was the best way to bring attention to my switch from the Democratic Party to the party of Abraham Lincoln to proudly become a Civil Rights Republican and to salute those great men and women buried at Woodlawn. Reviving the great Republican principles of freedom, opportunity and personal responsibility are the key to reviving the hopes and dreams of the current generation of black youth. It happened under the moral leadership of Frederick Douglass, Martin Luther King, Jr. and Abraham Lincoln.

Just this past Monday the Jack Kemp Foundation held its annual Awards Gala in honor of the late modern day Civil Rights Republican Jack Kemp. Kemp implemented these same principles to revive the hopes of a new generation of poor and black Americans. It was as the Secretary of Housing and Urban Development that Kemp's HOPE programs and enterprise zones provided both entrepreneurial opportunity and a path to home ownership, the American dream, to low-income Americans. With so many African Americans qualifying for these programs, Jack Kemp is still revered as one of the most popular politicians ever in the eyes of the black community. He once said, "No government has been able to do for people what people are able to do for themselves when given the opportunity." Langston and the majority of the 36,000 people buried at Woodlawn understood this and did not hesitate to jump any obstacle including fences to seize opportunities.

The question now becomes whether Howard University is still worthy of its reputation as the mecca of Historic Black Colleges and Universities. With the resignation of President Sidney A. Ribeau amidst declining enrollment and rumors of fundraising difficulties, one wonders if Howard has become a symbol of this lost generation? Maybe the revival of interest in the preservation of Woodlawn Cemetery is a sign of a new commitment to the principles of our great leaders of the past. Is it possible that an historic graveyard and not "The Yard" at Howard University will be the place where democrats and republicans, Americans of all colors, income levels and education can come together in a common effort to support the Woodlawn Cemetery Perpetual Care Association for the restoration of this treasure? If so, then the message to all Howard students and alumni is that you do not have to pay to get into this "yard" or jump the fence to have the privilege of standing on the holy ground of the final resting place of your black ancestors who want you to take control of your own story, your own history and pass it on to the next generation just as they have passed it on to you.

Chapter 4

Don't Take It to the Grave

Moe calls the thoughts that go into his writing "threads." Some overlap, some intersect, some follow up on the previous one.

After coming home from prison and spending time with civil rights pioneers Amelia Boynton Robinson, Annie Lee Cooper, Reverend James Bevel, and Reverend Orange—leaders who fought alongside Dr. King against segregation and in favor of voting rights—he took issue with D.C. politicians. Starting with Marion Barry.

"I loved Marion Barry, but one of my pet peeves against him was when I used to talk to him, I was like, 'Barry, you know, why don't you use this last quarter of your life to teach the young people what you know, because you know so much, I don't know of a more polished politician than you.'

"This is one thing that our Black leadership and Blacks in general have failed to do. People tend to go to the grave with a wealth of knowledge that they've learned from the movement, and from mistakes, and they don't share it with the next generation. The Marion Barry Leadership Institute at the Department of Employment Services does a great job, but Barry himself ... if people like him had really built the next generation to come behind them to lead, to grow what they've

I just think there's a lot that our leadership could have done better, and when the movement became less about the young people being involved, then the young people forgot all about the movement.

already sacrificed for, then we would benefit much more as a nation. If I had to look into some of the things that I think they could have done better, this was one of them."

Which brings to mind Peaceoholics, and lessons Moe learned the hard way, and then passed on to the next generation. Though the group had turned many lives around, mismanagement, unproven allegations and media criticism damaged his reputation, he says. Yet it made him stronger. "I didn't let the political-led attacks kill my spirit," Moe says, thankful for the support he received from the likes of D.C. Attorney General Karl Racine, for holding him accountable for bringing value to city-funded programs, and the "People's Lawyer," Johnny Barnes, for providing pro bono legal assistance.

"Thank God for them," he says, noting that he has received valuable advice from a number of diverse sources. "I was warned by a civil rights leader: 'It's not the 100 good stories, it's how you deal with the 10 bad ones coming your way.' Most of what was said about me was not true, but there are things I could have done better or people who I should not have trusted. Regardless, it all made me a better person."

I always was impressed by the way Moe has rebounded from the controversies, political battles, and media beatdowns and turned them into teachable moments. Those who don't know him well might have missed it, but I saw his transformation as it was taking place. Look, Moe can still create a spectacle, chew out a reporter, or publicly engage in political combat if need be. But instead of yielding to bitterness over his ordeals or affirming the negative public image some projected onto him, he channeled his energy into the Civil Rights Movement, and into passing his experience and enlightenment on to a younger generation.

He and I have talked many times about the value of turning conflict into opportunity to connect, as he did with me. Especially for young people, considering how quickly slights and beefs turn to violence that could be avoided if handled the right way. That's how he attributes his own growth—and that's how he attributes the growth he's seen in youths who are willing to listen when elders bestow their wisdom.

Sitting in the living room with Miss Robinson or sitting in Marion Barry's office with Winnie Mandela touched his soul, Moe says. It caused him to appreciate the value of learning civil rights history from his ancestors before they died, as they had done before him. "Who are the ancestors now?" he asks, criticizing modern leaders who don't use their political and social capital to educate youths who might look up to them, if given the chance. "So they can be greater than us. Some of the young people we took on these civil rights tours were gang members, but some of them got their master's at 25, some are advisory neighborhood commissioners, some of them are working for the Housing Department."

In early summer 2021, the *Washington Post* profiled Alexis Hawkins, a Peaceoholics mentee from Congress Park who graduated from Howard University Law School. These are people everybody gave up on, he says. "I just think there's a lot that our leadership could have done better, and when the movement became less about the young people being involved, then the young people forgot all about the movement."

Being part of that movement is a generational pursuit that requires learning what the struggle was all about, and appreciating the sacrifices of others, as a means of dealing with your own struggles. "How can they appreciate the value of what they don't even know about? We kind of dropped the ball on teaching the next generation about what we went through, and what their ancestors went through. We can't count on somebody else to tell our story. We should be doing that ourselves."

Moe recalls taking rival gang members who were beefing on a civil rights tour and coming back with them hugging and shaking hands. "That's how powerful knowledge is," he says. "Naive people tend to hurt each other. They don't know any better. When we teach young people certain principles we live by and certain things that humanity and organized civilizations live by—and how to fight against people who are your oppressor, you know, the right way—then you tend to make the whole society better."

Youths who came through his program would come back to mentor those even younger. "We changed their mindset, and when they would mentor other young people, they was like, 'Damn, that was me in middle school!' They learned from us how we dealt with them, so they knew how to deal with young people behind them. When we don't give them the opportunity to go and transfer that knowledge to the next generation coming behind them, then we do them a disservice."

"I learned so much from Marion Barry. Like when he told me, 'Don't take this shit so serious all the time. In politics you have no permanent enemies and no permanent allies. It's all about who's addressing your interest.' So, even when we didn't agree, know that if his leadership and thinking were better institutionalized in the final stages of his life, there would be an army of Moes as opposed to a squad. That's why I keep pushing."

When the Movement Forgot the Children the Movement Lost Its Power

Washington Post, May 10, 2015

By Ron Moten

Fifty years ago, a 34-year-old Dr. Martin Luther King, Jr. delivered his divine and historic "I Have a Dream" speech at the 1963 March on Washington for Jobs and Freedom. It saddens me to say this, but "The Dream" is not being fulfilled and I fear the movement is becoming powerless due to its lack of inclusiveness of young leaders and youth. In my eyes, many of the leaders who walked away from King's assassination with blood on their clothes let the movement die because over the following decades they failed to embrace, engage, and train new leadership. A perfect example right here in our nation's capital is Marion Barry who worked with and learned from not only Dr. King, but from other inspirational leaders such Rev. James Bevel, Dorothy Height, John Lewis and great freedom fighters in organizations like SNCC where Barry was the first chairman.

In 1965, at only 29 years old, young Barry moved to Washington, D.C. well educated and clear on his calling and purpose of uplifting America and the blacks he was proud to represent. One would think that leaders such as Barry would have made mentoring new leaders a priority, passing on what he had learned and how to use those skills to make even greater strides in the pursuit of freedom, equality and happiness in urban America. Just imagine if the children of today knew what Marion Barry knows. For instance, most urban American children and adults don't know the 1963 March on Washington was a direct result of the activism of black and White youth who participated in the 1963 Children's March which ultimately forced JFK to change his mind about civil rights issues as recently shown in the hit movie "Butler."

In April 1963, over 5,600 youth were beaten and jailed in their quest to end segregation and to run the racist Bull Connor out of Birmingham, Alabama. This youth activism which led to the Children's March was a catalyst for the elimination of Jim Crow laws. I often daydream about seeing Marion Barry in a classroom at Ballou Senior High teaching students that there is more power in direct action to uplift themselves and communities than there is being a leader of a gang or using a gun. One creates hope, the other destroys families and communities. After going to prison and attending college where I studied African American History, I returned home to meet and become a student of civil rights icons who worked with King and who were organizers of this historic children's movement of 1963.

It was because these great men and women were willing to mentor us that Jauhar Abraham and I were inspired to pass on what we had learned to youth who we mentored through our Peaceoholics programs. The youth of D.C. could have learned these same lessons directly from the legendary Marion Barry and other leaders who benefited in their youth from the Civil Rights Movement. Through our sharing this message we witnessed many positive results: Sharice Crawford who went to Ballou High School and graduated from Shaw University is an elected ANC in the impoverished Congress Heights Community where she was raised. Now she is fighting for and pushing the people to become self-sufficient just as Barry did in times past. Madina, Davina and Monica Watts from rival street gangs went together on civil rights tours and became students of icons like Amelia Boynton Robinson who is called the mother of the Voting Rights Act.

These same girls often visited her house just as King did when organizing on voting rights issues. These girls have gone on to be responsible for bringing about the truce between two rival gangs when they brought the boys to the table who we couldn't reach. This was vital in stopping years of violence that their communities had suffered from.

The girls learned from the likes of Pastor Gwendolyn Webb who was a child foot soldier in the Children's March. It's no accident one got a master's degree from Smith College at age 22. These lessons are so powerful, and it is tragic that the older generation of leaders has not passed their wisdom and skills on to our children. Lastly is the story of Maurice Benton who was shot and lost his intestines as a result of a gang beef between Barry Farms and Condon Terrace. He told his community not to retaliate because of the lessons we had taught him about the non-violence movement. The Dream started with youthful leadership and won't become a reality without an intergenerational movement in which the leaders pass the lessons of history to the youth before they take it to their graves.

Chapter 5

Black Women: Still the Power
Behind the Movement

This op-ed, published in the *Washington Post* in 2017, predates the viral ascent of the #MeToo movement by about six months and was actually inspired by the rise in reports of Black girls in D.C. reported missing or running away from home. That, and Mayor Muriel Bowser's promotion of an "Empowering Males of Color Initiative," including an elite all-boys high school, which sparked a discussion about gender inequality.

Moe felt chaos in the Black community was affecting girls as much, if not more than, boys, which spelled trouble, given key roles Black women played in the Civil Rights Movement, their frequent roles as heads of single-parent households, and increasing leadership roles in society. And though Peaceoholics helped guide many girls and young women, studies also show an increasing number of Black girls entering the juvenile justice system at a rate—not surprisingly—disproportionate to White girls. Even as I write this, we both are still reeling from the recent fatal carjacking of a food-delivery driver by two teenage girls down by Nationals Park.

> My grandmother, she's supposed to have been dead a long time ago. Strong women like that have got a fight in them you've never seen before.

Moe's relationship with women is complex. He was raised primarily by his grandmother, has never been married, and has multiple children by multiple women, one with whom he is in frequent conflict. He has two daughters: one that he co-parented with a friend-for-life he met at Howard during the youth mobilization of the Million Man March, is a recent graduate of Delaware State University with a degree in political science. His youngest, who has lived with him for the last year and a half, is an honor student.

Having been raised by an older, strong Black woman, his primary concern when he wrote this piece was that the Black community can ill afford to neglect the lives and struggles of its young women, much less leave them behind. "Especially now where the majority of the young men are being raised by young or older Black women," Moe says, "if the women are dealing with trauma without any support, we're not going to have those great women leaders like Dorothy Height, Gwendolyn Webb—one of my mentors—or Amelia Boynton Robinson, the mother of the Voting Rights Act."

That brings to mind the #MeToo movement, which has laid bare the omnipresence of trauma due to sexual harassment, Moe notes, and that has repercussions not just for female survivors, but for those they nurture, destabilizing entire families and communities. "The thing is, we've always had strong Black women," he says. "But the #MeToo movement at times puts checks and balances in place where everybody has to look at everybody as one, as equal. And when you don't have an equal society, all types of things can bring chaos to our community, where women are always advocating and fighting for the children more than anybody, which comes naturally."

Moe says he can attest to that from his own life experience with women, which enlightened him in multiple ways. "So I called upon both of my aunts when I grew up. They were prominent lawyers in D.C., two gay women. At the time I didn't even know what that was, because it wasn't accepted."

His grandparents had worked their way out of public housing and were able to buy a house in Petworth, he recalls, but they needed someone to sign for the loan, and his aunts stepped up. He says they treated him like a son: "They taught me how to be successful by working hard. I'd go up to the Gold Coast in D.C. around Carter Barron [Amphitheater] and Rock Creek Park and shovel snow and rake leaves. They would get me all the business and teach me a lot."

That didn't keep young Moe out of trouble, but the lessons stuck. Eventually.

"Dorothy Height and other prominent people would be in the house, someone would be playing the piano, they were networking and having fun. That was just my first exposure and my first glance of seeing powerful women. So I've always been exposed to women who gave you wisdom," Moe says, remembering his aunt, Gwendolyn Haywood, and her common law wife, Dovey Roundtree, a trailblazing civil rights lawyer who won a court battle for the Freedom Riders. Her name graces the Roundtree Residences, across the street from where she broke ground as a female pastor at Allen AME Church in Southeast D.C.

Mostly, though, Moe's grandmother raised him. He knew he could always turn to her. "She showed me what family was. I don't know what I would've done without that woman, because whenever I've gone through something, even when I lost my house, my car, I had that couch at my grandma's house to go lay on, you know what I'm saying? She never looked down on me. She never talked down on me. She was there for me. And that's what the woman has been to me."

The dual focus on respecting older pioneers of the civil rights era and nurturing Black girls and young women has reinforced Moe's belief in the value of instilling wisdom in younger generations. A young person will listen, if they feel the spirit of the person who is speaking to them, he says. This, in turn, leads to a form of empowerment, like Amelia Boynton Robinson, who was beaten on the Edmund Pettus Bridge on Bloody Sunday, and pushed in a wheelchair across that same bridge recently on the 50th anniversary of that sacred day—by Barack Obama.

"One of the things she said is, 'When your mind is telling you what to do, and your spirit, your intuition, is telling you what to do, listen. It is

God telling you what to do,'" says Moe. "And when she says this among children, you can hear her spirit, you can feel it, and they listen."

It's not just words that children notice, however: "My grandmother, she's supposed to have been dead a long time ago. Strong women like that have got a fight in them you've never seen before. Sometimes, when you're going through stuff, you think about what they went through, when they didn't have nothin' but a desire to be somebody. But they fought, and they made it, so I cannot give up, you know?"

Moe has seen what happens when elders lose sight of the problems and struggles of a younger generation: "More than 13 years ago we had that female gang problem in D.C., and we had to deal with them. I saw a lot of programs and a lot of females in negative situations benefit from those programs. But like I said, what happens so much is when the bad things go away, you stop doing the things that helped the children, and the negative things come back."

Internet content, video games, and even popular music have destructive themes that are influencing young Black women every bit as much as young Black men, Moe says, and in a graphic and virtual manner that is unlike what his generation experienced.

Again, it's a generational phenomenon that requires strong mentorship, in a gender-specific—and sensitive—manner: "So, if people who are trying to elevate these young women, if they can't take care of themselves, it makes it harder to mentor and guide this next generation of females, who a lot of times come from broken homes, or are guided by influences that don't mean them well, yet whose influence will impact young men like me forever."

Artwork: Michaye McIlwain

We Can't Keep Leaving Black Girls Behind

Washington Post, April 28, 2017

By Ron Moten

There was an uproar last month when an attempt by the Metropolitan Police Department to raise awareness about missing D.C. children was misunderstood. People thought the children were newly missing. They weren't—but they were missing.

This spurred talk about why girls of color get less attention when they disappear than White girls. That's a good question—because generally we are not focusing on girls of color. And that's a problem.

Soon after D.C. Mayor Muriel E. Bowser (D) announced the $20 million Empowering Males of Color initiative, which includes a new high school, some questioned whether it was legal to exclude girls from the initiative. One councilwoman filed a request asking for a legal review to see if it complied with federal Title IX laws that require equal public investments in girls and boys.

The law is not my expertise, but this is the right question to ask. If we continue to neglect the issues facing girls, the boys of color initiative is doomed to fail.

Peaceoholics, the antiviolence organization I co-founded, never could have squashed more than 40 major violent beefs in the District in its six-year run without the leadership of young women.

I fear that we are making a mistake in our fight for racial justice and equality if we exclude girls.

Those of us who do grass-roots activism can tell you that the challenges facing girls of color are just as serious as those facing boys of color. Only 12 percent of poor children live in two-parent households. That means the majority of our children in poverty-stricken urban areas such as Southeast are being raised by single mothers. If we neglect girls' needs and overlook their leadership potential, My Brother's Keeper will not get anywhere—those boys are being raised by women. We need to make sure those women are empowered, and we can't wait until they're grown.

Girls of color face their own challenges: Forty percent of sex-trafficking victims are black. The majority of women and girls in correctional settings have been victims of violence—domestic violence, rape, sexual assaults and child abuse. "Black Girls Matter," a new report by the African American Policy Forum and Columbia Law School's Center for Intersectionality and Social Policy Studies, highlighted the troubles facing black girls in school. They are often left out of efforts to end the school-to-prison pipeline. In Boston, for example, they have as many as 11 times the number of disciplinary actions compared with their White peers. They are the fastest-growing population in D.C.'s juvenile justice system.

In 2004, we started taking groups of D.C. youths to Alabama to study with civil rights veterans and learn the best antiviolence strategies to apply in the District. The boys and girls met Amelia Boynton, Annie Lee Cooper, Gwendolyn Cook Webb, James Bevel and James Orange. We learned that women were key to the victory in Selma, Ala. We learned that young ladies such as Webb made a difference. She was among the young women who persuaded the males not to retaliate when the police whipped, hosed and sicced dogs on protesters.

This history shows the power of women in the community.

We used a similar technique to bring about truces among rival gangs such as Lynch Mob and Choppa City.

We started with the young women—and they were no joke. Several were former gang leaders themselves and had experienced violence on a regular basis. However, the young women were willing to listen to us. After we got them to join forces, the guys soon followed—just as they did in the 1960s.

Spending time down South with civil rights legends was a life-changing experience for all of us.

I have been so proud of countless once-troubled D.C. girls who are now successful women. Monica Watts recently graduated from Benedict College in South Carolina and is now an ANC commissioner in Ward 8. She used to be in Lynch Mob. Davina Callahan, formerly of Choppa City, earned her master's degree at age 22 from the prestigious Smith College.

These women show that if we wrap our arms around boys and girls of color, we will be marching in the right direction.

Chapter 6

Trading a Sacred Vote for a Holiday Turkey

This piece for the *Washington Times* is an oldie but a goodie. Only Moe could take a free turkey at Thanksgiving and turn it into a critique of politicians and developers who patronize disadvantaged members of his community.

No one wants to see people go hungry, especially on a day that celebrates gluttony. The fact is, people in need, people in general, they'll take free shit when and where they can get it. And if a free Butterball helps feed you and your family and allows you to partake in a timeless American tradition, then there's no reason not to accept it, with gratitude. That is one of the reasons I like this piece. Moe is provoking you—and the people who are giving you that turkey—to regard charity in a broader context of what many communities really need.

> It's kind of offensive when you see politicians giving away a turkey for one day like they're doing something great. I'm not saying it's the worst thing in the world, but I think people would be better served by being empowered to go fish for themselves.

Not surprisingly, he also has reasons that make him inclined to question a Thanksgiving tradition, and that is Thanksgiving itself—at least from a Native American perspective: "I have mixed opinions about

Thanksgiving in its full context as far as the history of where it originated, even though it turns into something great about bringing families and communities together," he says in 2019, on the day after we had both stuffed ourselves alongside our own families.

"But fast-forward to this day, it's kind of offensive when you see politicians giving away a turkey for one day like they're doing something great. I'm not saying it's the worst thing in the world, but I think people would be better served by being empowered to go fish for themselves versus waiting on something that's going to go in their stomach today, leaving them in the same situation tomorrow. It's like you have somebody who's in a cage and waiting to be fed by somebody. You take people, and you put them in a situation where they're being pacified and enabled versus being empowered. To me, nobody's really getting pushed forward. I just think we can do better."

Moe's not blaming anyone for lining up for that turkey. He just doesn't like the idea of waiting for a handout from people who ought to be bringing more meaningful assistance to the community. And he doesn't like an underlying reality that no one really ever talks about: There's a false pretense to the Thanksgiving turkey giveaway. "It's like people act like they are helping a group of people, but really they're helping themselves."

Moe recalls when Ward 1 Councilmember Jim Graham (now deceased) boasted that he was giving away 650 turkeys at Thanksgiving. The catch was, you had to listen to Graham's speech first, which Moe felt was self-serving. "You had people trying to gather praise for their own political aspirations versus really doing this out of gratitude, or saying, 'I'm serving God.'"

Even worse, Moe says, Graham wasn't even paying for the turkeys. "You've got developers paying for this, in some cases the same developers who are pushing people out of the city," he says, shaking his head in disgust. "The same developers who are pushing people out of Ward 1 were the ones giving Jim Graham the turkeys!"

Moe wrote this in 2013, but it reminds me of something we talk about all the time these days.

"Gentrification," he says. "And I was talking about this word over six years ago. But I don't think the 'D' word—developers—always has to be a bad word. I know some good developers who don't just care about themselves, they care about the people. But I would rather see developers invest in workforce-development programs and things that will help some of these people get to work versus one day of gratification for a politician."

This is something Moe thinks small businesses do better than larger companies, in ways that encourage people to lift themselves up: "Small businesses, they try to pull people up. Most big companies don't have that connection to the ground. They have no intention of pulling the small people up. There are some who helped small businesses flower on their own, so they can help the people. But with this handout thing, people don't need a handout, they need a hand up.

"For the last 30 years, we haven't done a great job of empowering people to do for themselves. We have done a great job of pacifying people to say we did something, but in the meantime, the buildings and the skyline in D.C. is incredible. But can we say that the people who've been here when nobody wanted to be here have grown the same way? The answer there is absolutely no."

I remind Moe that we can't talk about giving out free turkeys without talking about four-term D.C. Mayor Marion Barry, who was famous for it, but who also is remembered for creating employment opportunities for the city's middle and working class.

"Well, one of the things I can say about Barry, even though he gave away a lot of fucking turkeys—I will say that he built a lot of people up, like a lot of people in this city. All you had to do is work hard."

The Real Price of a Free Turkey from D.C. Politicians

Washington Times, November 28, 2013

By Ron Moten

Thanksgiving is a great American tradition that brings families together. For most people it means standing in line at the local grocery store to buy a turkey and all the side dishes and desserts that make for a memorable holiday. Unfortunately, there are many families who cannot afford to buy a turkey who yesterday got to stand in another line, not at the grocery store, but in the cold and rain outside of Union Temple in Southeast D.C. It is good that those families will be able to have a free turkey on Thanksgiving, but free is not really free.

Still, it was not easy watching them stand outside shivering and rain soaked as they waited. A story about two lions came to mind. One lion wakes up each morning in the jungles of Africa and has to find food for his family. The other lion wakes up in the National Zoo and has everything provided for him and his family in exchange for being caged up and stared at by visitors at the zoo. Both are lions, but only one is a king! When government helps people, it should be in ways that make them strong, independent kings and queens, not photo ops that put them on display to advertise the so-called good deeds politicians do to get votes.

Take for instance D.C. Councilmember Jim Graham boasting on twitter that he is giving away 650 turkeys to citizens in his ward. The thing that is so sad and insulting is it appears he was using the turkeys as campaign outreach rather than a simple act of generosity and gratitude. As it turned out, the turkeys were not sold for money, but neither were they free. Seems like even at Thanksgiving politicians have to exact a price for helping people. Graham made that very clear when he told those waiting in line, "I won't give out any turkeys until you hear what I have to say."

His speech was not about how thankful he was to have the privilege of representing them, but to make sure everyone would know to be thankful to him when it comes time to vote again. Even that idea is disingenuous, Graham did not pay for the turkeys, the developers who are making millions by pushing the people in line out of Ward 1 with their "bulldozer gentrification" gave Graham the turkeys so that he could buy their votes. Development is good when the long-time residents can enjoy the benefits and not just get bought off with a turkey.

Buying votes by giving away turkeys bought with money from developers who want to stay in your good graces hardly honors the meaning of. If Graham and other politicians who resort to these cheap stunts to obtain votes were really motivated by the plight of hungry people, they would be announcing a plan to provide jobs and skills training for the other 364 days of the year. What if the focus was to set a goal that by next November half of these families would be employed and be standing in grocery store lines rather than waiting in the rain and cold to hear Graham announce his bid for re-election?

Graham and Marion Barry, who gives out 2,000 turkeys each year, are making Thanksgiving a more joyful day for many people, but just imagine what would happen if the developers who put up the money for the turkeys, came out from behind the politicians they are courting and followed the lead of the locally-based Marriott Corporation and supported programs like "Back on Their Feet" that empowers D.C.'s homeless with job training and physical fitness? That would be a Thanksgiving tradition that results in families waking up on the Friday after Thanksgiving with something to really be thankful for, a job and better health, rather than just the memory of having stood in the cold and rain because some politician believed in one-turkey-one-vote.

What if the City Council's Thanksgiving gift to qualifying applicants was a one-year free vendor license with locations where they could get discounted rent as long as they live up to certain standards? If we can spark growth by giving developers tax subsidies and selling them million-dollar buildings for one dollar, why can't we do things like this for the poor instead of pacifying them with turkeys while those same developers take the land they have owned or rented for generations? The government taking land away would sound familiar to Native Americans. The great community activist Yango Sawyer said that one day is better than nothing but giving a man or woman an everyday job is better than one day of giving out turkeys.

How can we make people feel like kings even when they have to accept free turkeys for Thanksgiving? First, get them out of the cold and rain. Second, make sure the turkey is the least of what we do for people, not the most. Let's find them jobs, ease up on burdensome regulations, get them small business loans and grants. Third, let's tell the politicians that the real point of Thanksgiving is about gratitude to God, not to them and their developer friends who can't even let a man be a king or a woman be a queen for even one day without reminding them to be grateful to you, not to God.

Chapter 7

Community Economics

In this 2013 piece for the *Washington Times*, Moe goes back to the lessons that have informed his understanding of the Civil Rights Movement. That's his "special sauce" as a mentor: learning from his elders, applying knowledge to today's issues, and passing it on to the next generation. In this case, it was the quote from Nannie Helen Burroughs he used for his op-ed title that got his juices flowing.

What inspired you? I asked him.

"Wow. So I was watching TV, and people were storming the doors to buy the new [Air] Jordans, and I was just thinking like, over and over again, how we just take our money and spend hundreds of dollars on tennis shoes. Not saying if you like something, don't buy it. But I'm looking at the people doing it, and I know a lot of them can't even afford it. I also was thinking: What if all those people took their money and pooled their resources together and invested in something in their community where it can build some wealth, you know? And then I was just thinking about a lot of things I've learned by going down South, and learning about the civil rights movement, like through the eyes of Booker T. Washington and Nannie Helen Burroughs."

> Some people tend to think that something's gonna fall out the sky. And that's not how the world works in a capitalist society.

He points to a time, before segregation, when his Black ancestors developed skills and talents and worked extra hard to survive in a country dominated by White people. They had to innovate. They still do, he said, worrying that at the grassroots level, the spirit of innovation and hard work has faded away, as talents and energy get directed towards things that don't lift people up in a community sense.

"Some people tend to think that something's gonna fall out the sky," he says. "And that's not how the world works in a capitalist society."

Moe cites Black inventor George Washington Carver, who accepted an invitation from Washington to lead the Agriculture Department at the Tuskegee Institute and contributed to the invention of synthetic rubber. Wouldn't it be better to be the guy who helped invent the materials for the Jordans than to own them for yourself? Moe asks. Wouldn't it be better if communities pooled their resources and promoted self-sufficiency and ownership as a way to combat institutional racism, and not relent, as individuals, to consumerism?

"The same way our Jewish brothers and sisters did," he says. "They resourced their wealth, pooled their money together, bought businesses, bought products and created other products to sell, and supported each other by creating their own banks, their own airlines, etc. We have done it in the past, like in Tulsa and Rosewood, and it was destroyed by the undercurrents of America's racism. But we can't let that trauma stop us from bouncing back and doing it again."

Check It Enterprises is an example of exposing youths to the idea of ownership. Rather than relying on a government handout or the nonprofit system, the Check It crew leveraged the success of a documentary and created a for-profit retail fashion design business that also functions as a social enterprise.

But the founders of the enterprise did not stop there: The group now operates out of a storefront that the enterprise owns with the help of a $2 million city grant—a grant Moe and his partners earned by demonstrating a track record of business success and community services such as HIV testing, food bank, creative cultural space, and counseling; and by convincing city leaders of the potential of the group's vision, which includes booking community events, leasing business space, and launching the Go-Go Museum.

"And that's what we have to teach our people," Moe says. "Not saying everybody can do it. But a lot of people can—they're just not being given a blueprint or the motivation to do it for themselves."

Again, Moe notes, he takes guidance from his family members, who have been hard workers. If you know the man, he is all about hustling. Whereas in his youth he hustled drugs, as an enlightened person he has developed his own brand of hard work that I refer to as "the positive hustle."

"You just have to get in the right networks, be around the right people, and keep pushing," he says. "People gravitate to people they see pushing and trying. People move away from people who always have their hand out."

To Moe, hard work, creativity, and vision are all of a piece. "You have to be the person who comes with something to bring to the table. When you tend to work hard, you tend to create things, and when you create things, you tend to come up with a vision. That vision can lead to ideas that attract people who can possibly help you or your community."

Not everyone is cut out for it, he admits. Some people in his community who have been traumatized continue to feel like victims, which can become a psychological disadvantage to overcoming their pain. "Some people don't believe in our vision, can't see the dream. A lot of our children can't see that far. A lot of adults can't see that far. The people who sacrifice and take advantage of opportunities are the people who benefit and become bosses, become business owners and move forward in life."

As self-motivated as Moe is, he has a knack for recognizing potential and instilling values in young people—even gang members who stand atop a network of associates that number in the hundreds. It's about realizing a broader vision, he explained, making that vision accessible to those who are able and willing to gravitate to opportunity, and ensuring they have a path to move forward—and to then reach back to offer the help that they embraced.

"I'm talking about leadership, instincts, gut feelings," he says. "Like a lot of things that not everyone has. It's something about the skills that our children who come from communities that are broken have. They can be fixed by the very people who exist in those communities, if given an opportunity to take up a vision that is bigger than just buying a pair of tennis shoes, the most expensive clothes, or the biggest car. You get those things when you can afford them," he says, dressed as sharply as ever. "There's nothing wrong with living nice, because you only live once, as far as I know."

We Buy What We Want and Beg for What We Need

Washington Times, December 31, 2013

By Ron Moten

Watching and reading current news stories over the past week took me back to a quote by Nannie Helen Burroughs highlighted in my book Drinking Muddy Water. The quote is shocking but painfully true. Known and respected as a black educator and social activist, Burroughs said, "Black people buy what they want and beg for what they need."

Already in a deep spell of thinking about that quote, it was stunning to ride around town and witness firsthand many people who have little extra capital standing in line for hours to buy the $200 Jordan Gammas. It was unbearable seeing reports on the news and social media about the fights inside and outside of stores over an ugly pair of shoes that you cannot even shine back into shape after they are accidentally scratched if they get stepped on in the club or on a crowded metro train. A few months later that same ignorance of good priorities will lead many to buy another pair with money that could best be used to do more productive things.

This is exactly what Burroughs was talking about over 50 years ago but is even more prevalent today. Why? Because one hundred years ago there was a higher percentage of blacks determined to kick down doors to become engineers, scientists, doctors, lawyers, business owners, etc. It's a good bet that most of the blacks standing in line for those Jordans last week were unaware that the synthetic rubber used to make many shoes today was invented by a great black scientist named George Washington Carver. If a pair of rubber-soled shoes are worth fighting and dying over, is it any wonder that our youth will heist a car for a joy ride on its four rubber tires even if it endangers innocent people? It's tragic that the shoe buyers and the joy riders did not learn to focus on being producers rather than consumers like Carver whose inventions enhance people lives even today.

50

There was at least as much racism and economic disparity when Carver was achieving great things as there is now and many would say it was much worse in his time. So why is it that the aspirations of so many black folks are no longer to be inventors and business owners committed to building strong families and productive communities? It is because back then blacks bought into what Booker T. Washington said, "Our ability to make the world better depends entirely on our ability to make ourselves better."

Sadly, many of us who benefited from the accomplishments and great sacrifices of Burroughs, Carver, and Washington have become takers and have forgotten to pass on to the next generation the meaning of success, responsibility and purpose. Too many of us are the first to buy the bling we see in the latest rap video instead of building and rebuilding the institutions of success which made us a once proud community. We have allowed ourselves to be portrayed as people of government dependent broken families who value shoes over school and joy rides over freedom rides. Only Nike benefits from this mentality as it brings out the next shoe in its never-ending line of Jordans. Nike knows that people who can't afford those shoes will not only buy every new model but will stand in line all night and fight and die, if necessary, in an attempt to satisfy a void manipulated by deep insecurities that only a fool could honestly think a pair of shoes could fill.

Institutionalized racism is still an obstacle to be overcome and eliminated in America, but racism was not responsible for people standing in line last week to buy expensive sneakers as if they were in line for the last bus to heaven. Money is power and blacks are producing wealth for others primarily by being consumers rather than incorporating the art and skill of producing things. If the black community used its money in the right way, we would have more power and respect.

It is said that the collective spending power of the black community would make it the ninth wealthiest country in the world. There is no reason why blacks cannot change the economic equation in America, but only if we go back to the traditional values that got us through slavery and Jim

Crow and that fueled the Civil Rights Movement of the sixties. It begins with family and personal responsibility. The goal should be to rewrite the words of Nannie Helen Burroughs to read, "Blacks buy what they need and build what they want." Then the future would look like this:

- Parents would line up for their children's PTA meetings like they do now for the new Jordans.

- Citizens would line up for city council meetings and sessions of congress to insure the people who represent us create policies that elevate us and do not put a strangle hold of dependency and submission upon conditioning us to be satisfied with crumbs and not striving for prosperity.

- Communities would line up to start investment cooperatives in the very neighborhoods where we are being moved out by gentrification.

- We would honor the line that goes back to our glorious, but difficult past when obstacles like racism were overcome rather than used as excuses for failure to build strong families and thriving communities.

Ultimately, reclaiming the values of our past would produce a people to whom a pair of shoes is not a god because more value would be placed on the great gifts and potential the true God has blessed them with within. There is a saying "A fool and his money shall soon be parted." Let's start by not fooling ourselves into thinking that happiness and value can be found at the end of a line to buy a pair of shoes. Then let's walk proudly in the shoes of our ancestors, past family members and all those who made our world a better place.

Chapter 8

Outside the Gate Looking in—Again!

In 2019, the Washington Nationals made the entire D.C. region proud when the team posted a miraculous comeback season and capped it with a gutsy and historic World Series victory.

Moe rarely misses an opportunity to examine how major events relate to the Black community. In this case, for the *Washington Post* he wrote about not being able to go see the team play at Nationals Park because of what he calls 'ticketification'—the ugly cousin of gentrification.

"So I was thinking about how, as natives, we always talk about how we were here when nobody wanted to be here," he says to me. "We were still invested in the city and sticking with it, some of us. And then, when the boom came, it was like we got pushed out, or people forgot we did so much."

"Like Go-Go music—people don't know there would never have been a Ben's Chili Bowl without Go-Go music, because it was a Go-Go every day of the week. People used to leave the Go-Go and go to Ben's Chili Bowl. This was when people weren't really going on U Street, right?" Washingtonians of a certain age will recall that in the late '80s, early '90s, as the Washington Metropolitan Area Transit Authority was building the Green Line and U Street was under construction, Ben's was practically the only business to stay open.

> I heard Nats fans complain about how they can't get tickets for the playoff games and for the World Series, standing-room tickets were going for $1,000. I'm like, 'Wow, now you know how I feel, goddammit.'

"People forgot about those types of things," Moe says. "And so I heard Nats fans complain about how they can't get tickets for the playoff games and for the World Series, standing-room tickets were going for $1,000. I'm like, 'Wow, now you know how I feel, goddammit.' But I felt for them, 'cause I was like, 'You know, this is the exact same thing that natives had been talking about: We helped build this city up. We supported you when nobody wanted to support you, and then things started going well, and you be like: OK, move to the side.'

"So I labeled it 'ticketification,' you know, the same thing as gentrification, but with tickets. It's just like what's going on. We have to have a greater balance. Growth is good. Gentrification is just fine when good people and natives who get up and work hard every day have the opportunity to stay and empower future generations in the new D.C. And that's my whole thing: the contrast of the natives and the fans of the Washington Nationals who pretty much come from Maryland and Virginia. Most of the fans that come from the suburbs are people who I think make more money than the people from D.C., who also support the team.

"So now you get to see what a lot of people in D.C. are crying about, and you might say, 'Oh, just roll your sleeves up and suck it up and work hard and you'll be alright.' Well, I know people work hard, go to work every day, and they couldn't go to those damn games. I was like, that's what this story is about, you know."

He has a point. I live in the District, and I'm a loyal Nationals fan, but I can attest to the White suburbanness of the fan base. Yet at the World Series victory parade down along the National Mall, you saw so many Black Washingtonians out there with joy and pride. Which brings up another issue altogether: Wouldn't it be great to see more Black baseball fans at the ballpark, especially children? I always wonder why I rarely see Black fathers and sons or Black families at the park—or groups of Black kids, maybe sponsored by the city, or a nonprofit.

What if corporations had incentive to sponsor more Little League teams and trips to the ballpark? I'm sure it happens, but not so much as you'd notice. And our team is one of the most diverse in the league. (Coincidentally, Major League Baseball just committed between $100 million and $150 million to the nonprofit social justice organization The Players Alliance over the next 10 years, in an effort to increase Black representation in the sport.)

Moe grew up playing sports—soccer, football, basketball—and appreciates the bonding that takes place among players and fans alike. "Well, sports and music bring people together in love," he says. "But what you see is a reflection of what's going on in the country. You have these lavish stadiums that a lot of times are supported by the taxpayers, right? But the taxpayers can't really afford to go into the stadium, and that doesn't make any sense. I understand in D.C. the Nats really showed people can come together, united, and win. It showed the spirit of love. But the question is: How do we keep that spirit going beyond the ballgame?"

He was talking about building a team and a fanbase as a metaphor for building a community, but also was making an even broader point: "And that comes from people really analyzing: How do we build people up and invest in the people just like that stadium? Like they invested in that stadium, I would say, let's invest in people, let's help people build businesses and build things that can remain, you know, brick and mortar. We had a conference recently with 50 entrepreneurs at Busboys and Poets, and I asked, 'How many of you all have a company or business and you sell products or whatever?' Pretty much everybody raised their hand. And when I said, 'How many of you can afford to operate in D.C.?' probably like 10% raised their hand."

With Check It Enterprises, Moe wants to teach young people how to build wealth and how to give back to their community and the generation behind them. In 2012, the group started with a $10,000 mini-grant from the Far Southeast Collaborative and eventually obtained their storefront across from the Big Chair. Then they raised $70,000 without any government assistance to create an anchor business—and that was before the development boom in Historic Anacostia. Now, several years later, with the help of a $2 million city grant, they own the storefront and two adjacent ones and are poised to launch a Go-Go Museum and a multipurpose, community-based venue that will serve as a training ground and incubator for aspiring young entrepreneurs.

Someday, those entrepreneurs will be able to afford Nats tickets, and the people they employ through their businesses will, too. Even for a World Series game.

What Washington Nationals Fans and Native Washingtonians Have in Common

Washington Post, October 27, 2019

By Ron Moten

It seems like the entire region is celebrating after the Nationals' historic playoff run. But for many, that good feeling evaporated when we saw the ticket prices: $1,100 for standing room only. Even worse, many season-ticket holders did not get to purchase tickets, according to reports. I call this "ticketification"—the ugly sister of gentrification.

What a slap in the face to D.C. taxpayers who subsidized this state-of-the-art facility with more than $600 million. We saw the vision. We invested. We waited patiently. We sacrificed. We were loyal before it was popular. Now, we can't afford to be there for the celebration.

As a D.C. native, I can relate. Right now, my city is winning financially, but every day it gets harder for us to be there for the party.

I am a partner at an Anacostia retail storefront and cultural space called Check It Enterprises, formed by former gang members, who, despite the odds, still believe in the American Dream.

We are among many of the current and former business owners supporting the Nationals but who are not part of the fruits that come with the development. You have to ask, "Couldn't the city and banks also have invested in the people and businesses who were there first and made them a part of the prosperity we see there now?"

A similar displacement has kicked in in Anacostia, with two of our favorite establishments being forced out because of landlords who wouldn't sell the buildings to the renters or renew their leases. When Caribbean Citation and Cheers at the Big Chair got pushed out of Anacostia, it killed part of the culture. Children need to see that hard work pays off.

You have to ask yourself what we can do to make this revitalization work for everybody.

I hope the ticketification of the Nationals inspires native, long-term and transit Washingtonians to work together as a team, just like the Nationals.

I am still riding the emotional high of seeing the underdogs make it to the World Series after several disappointing stints in the playoffs. It is refreshing and inspiring, to say the least, especially after the team lost star Bryce Harper.

I believe native Washingtonians and newcomers can get that win. Our victory would be a city that shares equity and opportunity for all, preserving the culture fabric that still exists while simultaneously being improved by the new wave of millennials and development.

If we don't, somewhere down the line, many of us old and new Washingtonians might end up like John Guggenmos, former owner of the Town night club in Shaw. His club replaced a go-go-friendly called club 2k9 that was forced to shut down, in my view, by gentrification and unjust stereotypes. It was one block from Metro PSC which is the birthplace of the #DontmuteDC movement. The Town catered to a Whiter, wealthier, gay and more professional D.C. clientele in 2007. The same forces that allowed the gay club to push out the go-go club eventually pushed out the gay club. A decade later, Guggenmos was quoted in the *Washington Post* as saying, "Gentrification is a great word until it happens to you."

I invite Washingtonians new and old to join us at our Don't Mute DC—A Call to Action Conference on Nov. 16 in historic Anacostia. Let's work together as a team to brainstorm solutions and actions that lead to the change we all deserve and want to see.

Chapter 9

The Violence Beneath the Virus

Obviously, COVID-19 has permanently changed the way all of us think not just about life, but the world. The same problems remain, but in the context of a global pandemic they all carry a new meaning. Yet even with close to one million dead in the U.S. alone, there's at least one thing that is as tragic as any COVID-related death: violence, and in particular, gun violence.

Moe probably had something broader in mind with this op-ed for my website, *District Dig*, in that violence comes in many forms, but he indulged me because gun-related murders are up at a time in which the pandemic is affecting our behavior all over the world. "Well, I think you got a lot of people who really don't know how to control their emotions right now, and they do things out of anger," he says. "Whether it's somebody protesting in the streets, or a young person was mad because somebody said something wrong to them, or somebody blew their horn at them, they decide to shoot someone.

> How do we test the minds of people and move them forward during this virtual world, and prepare for a more hands-on approach when things open back up?

"I think this is where we're at in society. We have to deal with the mentality of people we're dealing with; the influx of guns into our community and into the hands of young people is definitely a serious problem. So if we're not trying to figure out how we deal with the psyche of people who are having these knee-jerk reactions, we're not going to change. How do we do that? How do we give them opportunities when they feel like if they get disrespected, it's so much to lose that they waste their life on taking another person's life?"

In early 2021, D.C. Police Chief Robert Contee III announced that his department would no longer be focusing on getting guns off the street as much as focusing on bad actors who have guns. Then the Department of Justice announced that the D.C. area would be one of five regions where it planned to launch a gun-trafficking task force. And President Joe Biden has proposed public safety initiatives such as hiring more police—a suggestion bound to aggravate progressives and the Black Lives Matter movement—but also increasing their role in community engagement.

Are these good policy decisions? I ask Moe, whose public safety views have always focused on individuals and their communities. "I agree with it if we really have a strategy and are making an effort that's going to help the individual," he says. "I tell people all the time that prison saved my life. I got locked up, my brother got killed a month after I got locked up, and one of my best friends got killed six months later. That was enough for me to say: When I come home this time, I'm not doing the same shit."

But he couldn't do it alone. When he came home, he benefited from outreach organizations like Cease Fire: Don't Smoke the Brothers and Sisters. In his own violence-interruption work, Moe also has dealt with people who have been hardened. Often, the damage is inflicted early on:

"I'll give you an example. Let's look at Stanton Elementary right now. Those young people have seen five of their friends killed over the last two-and-a-half years. I've worked with some of them, and none of them have received therapy. So this becomes their norm. And they become numb. And they don't feel this stuff anymore. So now, when they start inflicting pain on other people, they have no sense of what they're doing. We keep producing people like this by not solving those other problems. We need to make sure people who are traumatized and see all this death in the community get services. If we don't start dealing with that early on, it reproduces itself. So when you know this is happening, can you hold a person fully accountable for their actions? As you look at them, do you say,

OK, let's put a plan together to help this person heal and ensure that they don't hurt somebody else?"

I was curious whether the Black community sees the White community as having become numb to the violence as well.

"I don't think people really ever care about what is happening until it affects their quality of life," he says. "Because if they did, we could have dealt with the root causes. And that's never been the case. Or else we would not be dealing with mass incarceration and carnage in the streets. But if things start happening close to them and they start getting uncomfortable, then they have no choice but to care."

But that's not enough, says Moe, who looks at violence and society's problems as collective ones that require collective, proactive solutions. "I think everybody has a role to play. We need everybody at the table. Because we know in D.C., it's two different worlds. Whether it's education, health, or violence, we are talking about two different worlds. And it's been like that for a long time."

Moe works across racial lines, but he believes certain types of outreaches have to come from inside the Black community, which he never hesitates to analyze, if not criticize. "First of all, you have to have people who genuinely care about doing the work. When you start talking about dealing with violence, and being an interrupter, we gotta make sure that the people that we're empowering to do that are people who are really doing it from the heart."

He knows from experience that resources are there for groups like Cease Fire and Peaceoholics (when they were still together). And he knows that self-gratification or self-interest won't cut it: "If they're not doing it for the people, those people can feel that. Part of this work is spiritual, and when people can't feel your spirit, you won't connect with a lost soul who most people have already written off."

So in the context of our times, has the pandemic forced the youths into virtual learning situations that have made them harder to reach?

"Most definitely," Moe says. "I think like, virtually, we just have to figure out, how do we touch the hearts of people? How do we test the minds of people and move them forward during this virtual world, and prepare for a more hands-on approach when things open back up?"

Moe with youth mentees, Ed and Sonny, after interview on News Talk with Bruce Depuyt. Ed was recently killed by a stray bullet while home from college.

Pandemic to Peace: Affecting Social Change in a Time of Crisis

District Dig, January 27, 2021

By Ron Moten

The statistics make clear that Washington, D.C. experienced four-straight years of a decrease in murder, from 144 in 2008, to 88 in 2012. There were many reasons for this steady decline, including community organizations like my former anti-violence group the Peaceoholics. Our outreach workers and community influencers worked with youth in our troubled communities, schools, and rehabilitation centers to broker more than 40 truces and sent more than 160 troubled youth to college.

These accomplishments were part of a citywide, grassroots effort devised from the bottom up, and supported by city officials.

However, there is an intricate piece of the puzzle that we once again find ourselves trying to solve: There was an 81.8% closure rate in D.C. homicides in 2012 compared to 43% in 2020, according to the Metropolitan Police Department. One thing we know for sure is that non-rehabilitated killers will likely kill again.

Added to the erosion of the social fabric of our communities, and a troubling lack of moral compass in our businesses, is the increasing distrust of law enforcement and the escalating number of unjustified murders of Black people on a national level.

Our communities are undermined by the availability and commercialization of guns and addiction to hard drugs. And while billions are now spent on a losing battle against an opioid epidemic that is migrating from the suburbs into the city, we promote the burn out of our youth and young adult population with the lure and overuse of an expensive and addictive recreational drug called marijuana, without any form of preventive education in place. Sheesh, at least the casinos do it for gamblers.

These travesties have resulted in a justified and overdue movement in search of a social awakening. As Co-founder of Don't Mute DC, I fully support any effort to bring about peaceful social change. I have more than two decades of experience in this work that tells me we are walking in the dangerous and muddy waters of anger without a clear agenda.

Anger and outrage over the inequities in our society are warranted, but I see too many people just looking for a reason to be angry without a strategic agenda or effective leadership. This is counterproductive to finding solutions and achieving real and measurable progress in the violence reduction and social justice we had during those four years a decade ago—hard-won battles we took to the street with the kind of accountability on all sides that results in accumulated power over evil.

The solutions are not complicated. But they take grassroots and government cooperation, in both time and funding, which are. Think about it, there was a time in D.C. when we used our music and unique culture as exhibited by Go-Go bands Backyard and CCB to help us convince our young people and our brothers in the streets that "it's not cool to be a fool," and that "suckers can't squash a beef!"

Instead, an attack on our music, culture and our very existence in our own city threatened to disconnect young people from music that was a platform of great influence. Positive D.C. music was replaced by an overdose of negative rap artists like NBA Young Boy, who says the Draco— a high-powered weapon—is undefeated, and by other lyrics that encourage our youth and young adults to use hard drugs.

As it is, we already lost our battle against violent video games that we waged against the major game companies in New York City, more than a decade ago.

It's crazy we hear our radio stations run commercials saying, "Stop the Violence," while playing the music of lost souls like NBA Young Boy and his peers who are promoting violence and the use of drugs, even as we now see people kill and rap about shooting another Black man. When songs like that were about police and other citizens, the stations bowed down to the pressure to move it off our airways.

Some will say change starts at home, but such platitudes often ignore the reality that the home is affected by the community around it. These are communities that were destroyed by the crack epidemic and mass incarceration, where, in 91% of households with 15–17-year-old children, a single parent—usually a mother or grandparent—is responsible for child-raising.

Now, the COVID pandemic has made our schools go virtual, further exposing the disparities and residue of injustice and inequity. This has pushed disengaged youth onto our streets and resulted in a rise of homicides and carjackings. At least one middle school in Southeast D.C. has an 18% student retention rate.

People are about to see how important our teachers and schools are, as I witness firsthand more and more young people with idle time getting entangled in destructive behavior and mental health traps, to a point where many see no way out.

The pandemic has us all scrambling to keep our youth engaged with a positive outlet for their talents. Based on my work in the community, I am convinced we must build a positive platform that gets their attention, or they will find negative ways to seek it.

To those who are angry about the injustices we see all around us, I say, anger is not enough.

An encouraging sign of hope for 2021 and beyond is that we now have a Chief of Police that fits the profile Washingtonians have longed for, to lead us in the right direction. But that is not enough. The ball is in our court. We must move fast and be intentional in D.C. and in every American city.

Close your eyes with me and envision the tables being turned. Consider that in the almost 200 homicides in D.C. last year, 191 of the victims were Black, and seven were Latino, while just two were White.

Now open your eyes and imagine that 191 of those victims were White, seven were Latino and just two were Black.

Do not just be angry about such an impossibility in Washington, D.C. Do something constructive when you think about the resources that would be made available, and the refusal to accept the normalization of violence that would result.

Commit yourself—despite inequity, institutionalized racism and lack of accountability—to re-establishing a moral compass among ourselves that, along with financial resources from government and business, could allow us all, together, to turn back the clock to the decline in homicides of a dozen years ago.

Chapter 10

Connecting the Blue Dots

Police reform is on everyone's mind right now. The murder of George Floyd in 2020 was preceded, and has been followed, by similar incidents demonstrating a lack of regard for human life, particularly Black lives.

In spring 2021, the D.C. Police Reform Commission found that the city is over-reliant on the police and recommended a greater investment in communities and in violence-interruption programs, which is right in Moe's wheelhouse as a champion and provider—as well as a critic—of such services. The commission also called for limits on cops' authority to search homes, frisk pedestrians, conduct traffic stops, interrogate children, and make arrests. But a crucial aspect was somewhat lost in the dialogue: The lack of local police who have meaningful ties to the city and communities they serve. Basically, not enough D.C. police come from, or live in, the District of Columbia.

> When you bring in people who don't understand the culture and the people in the city, you're setting the department and the people up for failure.

Moe grew up in Petworth, a northwest District neighborhood, at a time when police were well acquainted with the people who lived there. They may have gone to the same schools, or churches, or had relatives who did. That's not the D.C. we live in now, he says.

A positive sign, however, is the confirmation of Chief Robert Contee III, a native Washingtonian who grew up in Carver-Langston and attended public schools, and who faced the same problems many Black residents still face, such as drugs in their homes and violence in their neighborhoods. "From the perspective of a Washington native, I think [Contee's hiring] is a good thing," Moe tells me in March 2020, out by the Pirate Ship—that day we ran into one of his former mentees. "Sometimes you need an example to give people hope. He's an example that you can have a parent on drugs, and violence in your community, and you can climb your way out of that to the top of the police department."

In this op-ed for the *Washington Post*, Moe took issue with the requirement, implemented years ago by former Chief Charles Ramsey, that officers with the Metropolitan Police Department (MPD) must have at least two years of college credit to join the force. Recruitment is tough enough these days, especially among locals as Moe pointed out. But such a requirement disqualifies many young men and women who might be inclined to serve in communities they grew up in. Plus, he found it discriminatory.

"I think it's an oxymoron. You're making it seem as if the majority of intelligent people in the world have a college education, which is not the case. If you chose to go to college and utilize that for your advancement in the police department, that's one thing. But to just scratch people out because they didn't go to college, that's a bad decision. That's bias."

It's not that the MPD lacks Black officers; more than half of its sworn officers are Black. But the total number of officers is the lowest it has been in decades, and regardless of race, the likelihood they come from D.C. is low—as is the likelihood that they live in the city. In the most recent recruiting class, a 2021 *Post* article reported, nearly half of the recruits were White, with all but five coming from outside D.C. Four of them live in the city, and just one was born here.

Moe recalls growing up during the Marion Barry era, when the MPD had 65% Black officers—a good number coming from D.C. or surrounding areas. "We didn't always look at them as somebody who was coming to lock us up. They were the ones taking us to football games and basketball games, football practice. If stuff wasn't right, they called our parents. They weren't scared of the community, because they knew the community, and the community knew who they were. Some things changed when the crack epidemic hit, but still, we had some police who understood. It wasn't all about locking us up."

Because of changing demographics though, "the police force stopped looking like the city," says Moe. "And it stopped having people who understand the city. When you bring in people who don't understand the culture and the people in the city, you're setting the department and the people up for failure."

In fact, the *Post* story angle was that the current recruits—31 in all, from places like Florida, Indiana, and Wisconsin—had to undergo implicit bias training, learn about D.C. cultural history, and tour the National Museum of African American History, among other cultural-awareness activities. The department knows it has a problem, but it is trying to address it. The dilemma is that being police means being an outsider, someone the community mistrusts, which hardly encourages young people to become cadets, Moe says. And there's another dilemma: The cost of living makes it hard for new recruits to live in or near the communities they will be serving. As officers, they will be more likely to head to the suburbs when their shift is done.

In spite of these challenges, Moe has high hopes that as a native son of the city, Contee will demand more community involvement from his officers. The "community policing model" has been tried before with mixed results, but even as a less-rigid model, he sees value in it. "If the community policing component is put back in place, which Contee says he is trying to do, we will see. The thing about Contee, I think he listens. A lot of people always try to over talk people in the community versus listening. Even when you feel like the community is wrong, sometimes you've just got to listen."

The other thing Moe likes about Contee is that the chief is visible, and he knows the history of the Officer Friendly program of the 1970s and 1980s, which had faded away but was brought back in 2018 to help bridge the gap in perception between cops and communities. While Contee is as visible as his predecessors, Moe sees the chief's finger on the pulse of the city in a low-key manner as well. "I've seen him in the community already, even in Anacostia I was walking to work one morning, and I saw him sitting in the car with the mayor, unannounced, looking at what they're going to do right there. To me, that means a lot when you're hands-on, just observing so you can see what you got to do with your job. And that's what it's all about. You got to be a part of the community."

Re-examining the college requirement would be a bonus, Moe says; it would allow MPD to cast a wider net and offer career opportunities to young men and women who might want to serve but are currently not eligible. "In the past, I think many people on the force got diverted from negative behavior and went the other way and became a police officer. They were one second away from prison or got in a little trouble when they were children and changed their life around because they had a mentor. Sometimes the mentors were police officers. Not officers who think they have a license to kill, but a license to help and heal."

We Must Restore the Community Pipeline
to the D.C. Police Department

Washington Post, February 5, 2021

By Ron Moten

For a more than two decades I've said that former D.C. police chief Charles H. Ramsey, now a frequent guest expert on talk shows, made one mistake that would affect people of color and the effectiveness of the police department in our community for some time to come. As reported in the *Post* in June 1998, Ramsey changed the educational criteria for new police officers even though previous chiefs with great honors didn't. When he changed the requirement from a high school diploma or equivalency to a college degree, he effectively and severely reduced the number of new officers in the pipeline from the community.

I was critical of this policy from the beginning because I knew from personal experience that police officers recruited from our own communities have the most empathy and cultural competence to implement true community-based policing. Ramsey's decision was based on real concerns, but better vetting procedures and training would have addressed those issues without reducing recruitment from our neighborhoods. Having a police force without a connection to our community creates a disconnect that can be counterproductive to the spirit of community policing.

Fortunately, D.C. still produces quality people the likes of acting D.C. police chief Robert Contee III. His emotional speech about being nominated for D.C. police chief touched our hearts. He shared his journey from growing up in D.C. during the crack epidemic and watching a parent use drugs to being nominated to be the police chief of a major metropolitan city. Just a few weeks later, he led some of D.C.'s finest in defending our Capitol and protecting our democracy.

Many of us know from being in the streets that there were racist cops in the D.C. police and other law enforcement agencies around the country.

The *Post* has reported on a D.C. officer wearing a White-supremacist symbol.

This is why I was devastated and so angry when our D.C. Council bowed to pressure to kill additional funding for the MPD Cadet Corps. The program was to be expanded to Anacostia High School, which sits in a part of D.C. that has grown to distrust the police. The proposed expansion would have given a real opportunity to more than 200 young adults in a city with one of the biggest wealth and employment disparities. Graduates of the cadet program, which is mostly made up of minorities, tend to stay with the D.C. police. They serve and protect their own community and help today's youths make it out of situations that they barely did. These young adults become police officers who bring their personal experiences, love of the community and connections to youths who are experiencing trauma.

I differ on these issues with some of my friends at Black Lives Matter DC and on our D.C. Council, all of whom I respect. I have tried to explain to them and many of the young people I work with in the Don't Mute DC movement that this is about strategy and assessing the big picture. We must work together if we want to solve the problem of institutionalized racism that much of America has denied for far too long.

It's time to have some hard conversations on these issues and implement the solutions with real action. We must restore the community pipeline to our police departments and other first responders and challenge the institutionalized racism that has penetrated them for too long. The cadet program did just that.

We must be relentless about eliminating policies and opportunities that give racist people permission to inflict pain on people of color and corrupt the institutions that are supposed to govern and protect us. We can't do this with knee-jerk responses. Only a well-thought-out strategy will address these entrenched problems.

We have the right to be angry, but we should not be destructive.

Chapter 11

Numbing Down the Numbers

Manipulating statistics to downplay the extent of violent crime is what a reporter would call "juking the stats." If city officials can categorize some homicides as something other than murder, then maybe the public won't be as alarmed.

In this 2015 piece for the *Washington Post*, Moe aimed his critical lens at D.C. Police officials for trying to lower violent crime rates by including categories that were in decline and declaring that the "overall crime rate" is down. "It reminds me of when I first started doing this work for Peaceoholics," he says in our first interview, August 2019. "Initially, it was somebody who came and asked me to have our young people do a study or a survey and they came with all this data that they got from somewhere else, and our children were like, 'We don't know where y'all get that data from, but that's not our reality.'"

> We don't know where y'all get that data from, but that's not our reality.

If I've learned anything, it's that the word on the street according to Moe is closer to the truth than the government would have you believe. "I always believe that people who take data, they take it to make it say what they want to say. If they're looking for a certain answer, they'll go to somebody they can get their answer from." He is not alone in questioning statistics. "The numbers don't lie," in itself, can sometimes be a lie, in this reporter's view.

"Right!" he says. "I watch how we will always see these reports go out. Overall crime is down, this and that. When they say 'overall crime' is down, it's just like ... to me, it makes your blood boil."

I've never known Moe to joke about such things, yet I had to laugh when he responded to my query about what "overall crime" even means. "'Overall' means that I put enough things in the equation so that I can minimize the effect of what the real problem is."

The man has a way with words.

Basically, what he refers to is when officials take the rate of increase in violent crime (including murders, homicides, and rapes) and mix in the rates of lesser crimes (robbery, burglary, breaking and entering) that might be decreasing—or just increasing at a reduced rate—and claim that overall crime is down. It's a common rhetorical device that politicians have been using for years, Moe says. "That's what is alarming and brings about the illusion that things are better, when they're not better. And it was very discouraging to see people play with numbers and data like this. I couldn't let that go. I had to talk about all the cherry-picking of what you want to put in the data."

Just this past May, amid a 2021 homicide surge that reached a 16-year high for D.C., Mayor Muriel Bowser emphasized that burglaries and street robberies decreased last year—across the District—while shootings and car thefts increased. Then she told the *Post* that during last year's summer anti-crime initiative, "selected areas" saw a 10% decrease in violent crime and 25% reduction in "overall crime" compared with the summer of 2019. It's a form of spin to make a bleak picture look less bleak that Moe says he has observed for the last 25 years, regardless of who is mayor.

Even the media is complicit in downplaying crime in D.C. Last July, the *Washingtonian* magazine reported that statistics for 2021 do not show an appreciable increase in violent crime from 2020. This not only ignores the fact that D.C. has seen an alarming increase in carjackings since 2019, but the city also recorded more homicides in 2020 than in any year since 2004 and surpassed that number by 14% in 2021. To this reporter's eye, such reporting belies a stunning lack of sensitivity to how violence affects the collective psyche of the communities that suffer from it.

Such massaging of the facts also bothers Moe for other reasons, he says, because Peaceoholics had success in keeping people from shooting each other so often, whereas in his view, subsequent anti-violence efforts have not built on that success. "I had to write about it because I knew that violent crime was going back up, after doing the work that we did that started the decline of violent crime in D.C. for four years."

His point is, reducing violence in the community is as much an art as a science. Numbers don't tell the whole story—not where lives are concerned. "What people don't understand, it requires developing relationships and skill sets all over again, but with new people involved. So it was like they threw the baby out with the bathwater and tried to cover it up with a fake analysis of the data, compared to what was going on in the community."

Squashing beefs between rival crews is just one part of what Peaceoholics did, says Moe. From one generation to the next, they identified root causes of violence to prevent it and to steer people toward a nonviolent life. That could involve a job, vocational training, behavioral health care, or something simple but powerful that some kids never had: Love. "Anybody with common sense knows violence is going to reproduce itself and come back if we don't finish solving the problem. So when you get people giving the illusion that things are better, it gives a justification for not going back and fixing the root cause of the problem. Like, 'Hey we all right now, we don't have to worry about anything no more.'"

The consequences can be serious. Moe points to the shooters at the Caribbean Carnival up on Georgia Avenue some years back. "We took the shooters, put them in the school, got them to pull the neighborhood in and do conflict resolution and empower them to be the change agents and stop all the shootings up there that were going on." But once such intervention dries up, trouble resurfaces, he cautions. "The young men we got to squash beefs went from doing positive things to getting locked up for robbing a bank together, an armored truck."

Officials deflect the real situation in various ways, Moe says. A former police chief, Cathy Lanier, used to attribute the increase in homicides to domestic, or "personal," disputes—which might just as well be beefs between rival crews who are engaged in criminal activity in the first place.

One thing for sure, though, is that the police know where to study the problem. A 2021 report showed that all of the homicides in D.C. occur within the same 151 city blocks, just 2% of the total block number.

"Nobody wants to really let people know how many shootings happen every day because they think people are gonna be afraid," Moe says. "If we really look at the shootings and where they were and how they were happening, then I think we will be attacking the problem much differently. If you don't know who's involved with the root cause of the problem, how you going to solve it?"

Hiding the Truth in Overall Statistics

Washington Post, January 18, 2015

By Ron Moten

When I watched speeches full of cherry-picked data celebrating decreases in crime and increases in employment during former D.C. mayor Vincent C. Gray's (D) administration, I questioned what they were seeing that I wasn't. The new data-based assessment is that "overall violence is down."

The key word is "overall." A closer look at the data shows that crimes that matter most to our communities have gone up over the past two years, even though "overall" crime has gone down.

Let's look at the data. According to the Metropolitan Police Department, something historic happened in 2012. The 88 homicides in the District represented the lowest number of homicides in 50 years. We know now that 2012 would mark the end of four straight years of a declining homicide rate. In 2013, the number of homicides rose to 104. Some attributed the increase to the Navy Yard massacre perpetrated by a mentally ill man from Texas, so, in some ways, it is fair to say the District had 92 homicides that year. In 2014, the District had 105 slayings.

That is what the word "overall" is intended to cover up.

Politicians use the "overall" claim to hide increases in all sorts of crimes in the neighborhoods where I engage citizens every day. In some parts of the District, sexual assaults, armed assaults and domestic violence have increased, and neighborhood crew and gang activity has reemerged. Robberies and burglaries have decreased in most police districts, significantly in some.

Just think how things would look if the city released data on how many people were shot yearly—not just on how many died. Eight people were slain in one week last month, but there were 15 attempted murders. If this continues, the District easily could see the miserable 1980s homicide numbers return.

How does this happen in a diverse city with so much prosperity?

When I walk down Good Hope Road or up Martin Luther King Jr. Avenue in Southeast, I see countless 14- to 24-year-olds on the corners. They're unemployed or school dropouts. Many say they cannot find jobs or that they don't have the skills for the "new" District. Some plead for help in finding employment; some simply have given up. These are the data that matters.

It's no wonder our politicians can't come up with a decent plan of action when they don't even acknowledge that data. How could the former mayor brag about the decrease in unemployment when the rate for youth is extraordinarily high and the rate for former prisoners is stuck at nearly 50 percent? Many believe that the claimed drop in unemployment is mostly because of the 100,000-plus new Washingtonians who arrive here with jobs.

To solve a problem, we have to acknowledge the problem, look at root causes and find solutions for implementing a holistic plan of action. Four years of fewer homicides lulled District leaders into a false sense of security and lack of vigilance in providing the kinds of programs that reduce violence.

The increase in the crimes that matter to us most is not a strike against D.C. police, which have kept people safe by doing things such as shutting down the majority of the city's open-air drug markets. This is a collective problem. We must get creative. When we take the drugs out of a person's hands, we must replace them with skills that create employment opportunities or that help turn illegal hustlers into legal hustlers called entrepreneurs.

I also am not throwing a jab at the community; we have been very active in addressing unjust police killings in the United States. However, we must work with the same passion to address the violence we inflict upon each other in our community.

If we don't, the data—and our quality of living—will get only worse.

Chapter 12

Trust, Mistrust, and Trauma

Moe is an elemental thinker. He's always focused on root causes of crime and violence—and, of course, solutions.

In this 2015 op-ed in the *Washington Informer*, an important, female-owned voice in D.C.'s Black community for more than 45 years, Moe expounded on an expression I have heard him use many times regarding violent offenders: "Hurt people hurt people." In this piece, however, he also looks at it from the perspective of police and community leaders. "I was working for the Jack Kemp Foundation, and we were trying to resolve some of the conflicts that we see in most major cities throughout the United States, between the police and people of color," he tells me as we chat on the day after Thanksgiving 2019.

> There has to be a system put in place where people can have conversations.

The foundation was bringing together the two groups, he explains, organizing basketball games between returned citizens and the police, and moderating panels on mental health and discussions where both sides were encouraged to really listen to the perspectives of the other. According to Moe, people on either side of those discussions have ample reason to harbor distrust because of the physical or even mental pain they have been through, sometimes at the hands of the other. The key is getting both sides to recognize the humanity in the other, and understand they are having the same human reaction to the harm they have experienced. Only then can you expect someone you are at odds with to come with an open mind about their own mistakes or vulnerabilities: "I have a perspective that a lot of people don't see. And one of the things I've always been taught is, if you don't look at things in a balanced way, then you're not going to have any accountability. You're not going to have anybody buy into it from both sides."

The alternative, he says, is that people on opposite sides of the justice system continue the vicious cycle that can lead to the kind of civil unrest that has reached a feverish peak in the past couple years. "A lot of times the police don't hold their peers accountable, and the community sees that. So, if we don't create an atmosphere where, one, justice is going to be served and, two, people can have conversations where they don't necessarily always agree, we can't come to a resolution in dealing with these issues."

Moe likes to focus on archetypes to make his point. In this case, one of them was a no-nonsense cop named Buck, who worked at Ballou High School. If Buck locked you up, he recalls, the students would be the first to tell you it was because you deserved it. Buck also is representative of people in the community who "practice citizenship," Moe says—it's an expression of his that I have lifted on occasion to describe what I do as a journalist. Only, in Buck's case, instead of reporting and writing stories to inform the public, he takes a hands-on approach to engage with the children in the community so they can develop relationships with the police that aren't rooted in fear and mistrust, Moe says.

Much of it starts with overcoming specific incidents that had lasting effects. Buck has sustained serious injuries over the years even while trying to help people, says Moe; someone even spat in his face once. "Now, if somebody who's not culturally competent, or has no connection to the community right away, they might have reservations about helping people next time something happens."

By "cultural competence," he means the ability of police to see past negative aspects and assumptions of their relationships with Black people that have occurred so persistently since the days of slavery: "When you're culturally competent, even though you might not have been through what those persons have been through, you understand how they might be doing some of the things they be doing, which gives you the perspective that you're going to still do your job, but you also gonna try to prevent things before they escalate. That skill doesn't develop overnight."

It's a simple but logical philosophy, which is the best kind, in my view.

"There has to be a system put in place where people can have conversations," Moe says. "I think one of the biggest problems in our community, period—whether you're talking about police-community relationships, whether you're talking about Democrats and Republicans, no matter who you're talking about, Black, White—is that people just try to force the issues down somebody's throat. And that there's only one right way. When you get people to sit down and break bread and talk and say, 'Look, we're gonna leave out of here with something that's positive and everybody's coming to the table like that,' it's a lot different than, 'My way is the best way,' or, 'You're just a bad person.' And I think we have to get back to conversations like that, where it's honest but not from an argumentative or attack mode, where it's people can agree or disagree but can come to some level of understanding of each other. And when you do that, then you can start healing."

Amen to that.

Not Just in Baltimore, Hurt People Hurt People

Washington Informer, April 28, 2015

By Ron Moten

On January 15th, 2015, in recognition of Martin Luther King, Jr.'s birthday, I joined forces with Community of Hope Church in Suitland Maryland, the Jack Kemp Foundation, WPGC Radio and Prince George's County Police Department in holding a focus group on police and community relations. At the beginning, there was hostility by some of the young people towards the police and some defensiveness from the police officers who attended. There was a big difference between the controlled verbal hostility that night and the riots of uncontrolled violent hostility going on in Baltimore this week.

The main reason one confrontation between community and police is violent and the other productive is that at our meeting, both police and community felt like their grievances and frustrations had been listened to by the other side. The key was a skillful moderator who encouraged both sides to be completely honest when speaking and to give total attention when listening. It was hostility expressed in an environment of civility that made all the difference. When people who have been hurt, whether police officers or community members, don't think anyone is listening, there is a risk of lashing out. The first step to rebuilding trust is to make sure people hear people so that hurt people don't hurt people. Once there is even the smallest measure of trust, healing can begin.

All the good will and trust built up by the many positive things the police do to keep our communities safe can be broken with a single act of police misconduct. So when those young people came to the focus group carrying memories of negative experiences with the police, they weren't looking for explanations, they wanted to be heard. The same is true for the police, they go from one community meeting to another fatigued and frustrated that they are not being heard because the actions of a few make them all untrusted.

By the end of the event, the police and the young people were embracing each other, but not because they agreed on everything. They exchanged names and email addresses rather than tear gas and rocks because they felt listened to and that laid the groundwork for real outcomes to be produced by similar events in the future.

I have watched protest marches, leaders condoning by their silence the looting of stores and the destruction of property. I have heard police union representatives make remarks that have inflamed the citizens who in turn have set the city aflame. What has not been prevalent is honest dialogue in an environment of civility and acceptance that leads to outcomes that address concerns on both sides. Good citizens do not want to fear the police simply because of the color of their skin and good police officers do not want to be labeled racists when they are fairly and impartially doing their duty.

The lines of intolerance should not be drawn between good citizens and good police officers, but between those on both sides who do what is right and those who do what is wrong whether as citizen or law enforcement. When good citizens are treated unjustly and bad cops escape justice, tempers boil and blood is spilled. The way to get citizens and police constructively engaged is to have a proven process of healing in place that both prevents conflict before it starts and de-escalates it afterward. The key is to provide a pathway to healing for both the police and the community.

A rally at a church or some other public gathering place without a plan for healing, positive outcomes and accountability at the end of the tunnel will only lead to more of what we have seen in Ferguson and Baltimore. As Martin Luther King, Jr. said, "Riots are the voice of the unheard." That is why we must have systems and a process of healing set up to deal with the decades of pain which have plagued too many American generations.

We must be honest about the perception of many children of color that all men in blue are against us. We must be honest and teach our children that police have a hard job and can be desensitized with the many negative encounters some often experience even when trying to do the right thing.

The process starts with listening to each other and ensuring accountability, but listening is a skill, it is not natural to truly listen to those with whom we disagree. We are always trying to "fix" the problem, to lecture or accuse or become defensive. Our Kemp Forum on Police Community Relations events teach both sides to listen, not just to wait for the next pause to start talking.

Prince George's County is a great place for us to start because it was similar to Ferguson just over a decade ago. The county was plagued by excessive force by police. A *Washington Post* investigation led to the arrest and conviction of an officer for a series of K-9 attacks. A later investigation showed that from 1990 to 1998, 122 people were shot by police resulting in 47 deaths. In 45 percent of those shootings, the suspect was unarmed. That gave Prince George's County police a higher rate of fatal shootings per officer than any other major city at that time. This led to a Justice Department investigation and to federal oversight from 2004 to 2009. They cleaned up what was once considered a corrupt police department. From 2010-2014 Prince George's County police shootings dropped to 14, a very significant decline.

One of the strengths of Prince George's County Police Department today is the constant attention to maintaining and improving community relationships. As much progress as they have made, the recent actions of a bad cop threatened to undo the trust that had been so carefully rebuilt in the last ten years. Their well-deserved pride in the progress they have made does not make them complacent. Their honest and on-going commitment to quality improvement through community dialogue makes them a great model for healing police-community relations across the country. We are proud to have them as our partners, not because they are perfect, but because they want to excel.

Martin Luther King Jr. left us with this, "People fail to get along because they fear each other, they fear each other because they don't know each other because they have not communicated with each other." Lack of communication and listening has led to the fear and hate we see throughout our country within certain parts of the community.

Reverend Tony Lee opened the doors at Community of Hope Church and thanks to Chris McGoff facilitating an environment of mutual trust, the police, youth and community left hugging and embracing each other. Subsequently, there has been further dialogue between Assistant Chief Craig Howard and some of the youth who attended, not because they agreed on everything, but because trust was born through listening. Hello, Baltimore, Ferguson, America and yes, the world, are you listening?

Chapter 13

The Rights of Citizenship and
the Wrongs of Snitching

In the spring 2020, on a windy but clear day out by the Pirate Ship, Moe and I thought it would be appropriate to talk about a subject that never gets old: snitching.

When he wrote this piece for the *Washington Post*, in 2007, Moe was irritated by misperceptions about what snitching is—and is not. "I thought, we gotta explain that there is a difference between citizenship and snitching," he says. "Nobody likes a snitch. The police don't like snitches amongst them. Politicians don't like snitches. People who have worked on jobs don't like people who snitch, right?"

The problem, he says, is people in the streets who

> Even when D.C. was the murder capital, if a person killed a 7-year-old, they already knew they might as well turn they selves in, because the street would take care of them if they didn't.

might have reason to avoid the police have placed a stigma on people who were "practicing citizenship" by seeking help from authorities to address crime and quality-of-life issues in their communities. "And then most of these same people, when they get in trouble, they will be the first ones to turn in their friends, to blame it on somebody else, and not take accountability for what they've done and just go do their time."

Black folks used to keep close watch over their own communities, says Moe, but the social fabric is not what it was for older generations, back in their day: "Even when D.C. was the murder capital, if a person killed a 7-year-old, they already knew they might as well turn they selves in, because the street would take care of them if they didn't. We had people who used to hold things in check, but we lost the community component of holding people accountable. We took the voice of the people who would normally say, 'Listen, we can't allow this in our community,' and we criminalized them for being citizens."

The risk of being too passive is equaled by the risk of practicing citizenship, he says, noting that it's easy to end up with a target on your back. "I feel like this is one of the biggest enemies of the African American community. Like if a neighbor calls the police and the police comes and knocks on your fuckin' door. You know, you're about to get this person killed or hurt or whatever."

Moe has had to defend himself on his position, he points out, and leaders before him have as well, when it wasn't popular within parts of the community. (If you've read this far, or you know Moe, you know he is not one to shy away from controversy, or to speak or act on his convictions.) "It took a lot of balls to write," he says matter-of-factly about this op-ed. "I mean, I got thousands of emails and responses. That found more traction than any article I've ever written in my life. And most of it was good, but I got a lot of people who responded to it who didn't agree with me, but that was good, too, because at least it sparked a dialogue that people weren't having."

That dialogue took place in an indirect manner when D.C. was grappling with the fate of one of its most notorious crime figures. In February 2021, after prosecutors made a case for leniency, a federal judge reduced the life-without-parole prison sentence of 1980s drug kingpin Rayful Edmond III to 20 years due to his two decades of cooperation that led to the successful prosecution of numerous drug and homicide cases. (Edmond, who turned 57 in November, has asked for a 10-year reduction in a separate 30-year sentence in federal court in Pennsylvania.)

The Edmond matter, which resulted in citywide town halls moderated by Attorney General Karl Racine, is a touchy subject for Moe: "I mean, people still love him, but he was a snitch. A lot of people went to prison. He decided to go to work [for the government]. A lot of people who were in his case didn't. And then you have his co-defendant, Tony Lewis."

Tony Lewis Sr., top lieutenant in the Edmond cocaine ring, was convicted of conspiracy to distribute cocaine in 1990 and sentenced to life in prison without parole. For years now, his son, Tony Lewis Jr., has led a "Free Tony Lewis" movement, arguing that his father's punishment long ago surpassed the seriousness of his crimes. Lewis Sr. had no prior criminal record and was never charged with a violent offense, his son and supporters argue; since being imprisoned, he has expressed remorse, been a model prisoner, and dedicated himself to community service and anti-violence advocacy.

"They gave Tony life for a nonviolent crime," Moe says, "but he still didn't tell on no one. He's been in for three decades, and he's still fighting to come home, even though he's been a model prisoner and has worked with his son to encourage young people to not follow in his footsteps."

Contrast the Edmond drug ring scenario with activists who try to resolve matters in the community before the police are even involved, Moe points out: "We live in two cities for real, so I think the first thing should be, how do I help people? You try to help people first, but some things require a person who is not in the streets to call the police, because some people in the streets might have to go to jail to be saved. A lot of citizens have trouble with that, turning someone in to what they see as an unjust system."

I lay out a scenario in which someone knows someone who has an illegal gun. What, if anything, should they do?

"I think if you know somebody has a gun, and they are showing behavior as if they're jeopardizing public safety, or like they're going to harm someone, you have an obligation to protect your community first," Moe says, indicating that informing the police would be appropriate under those circumstances. That's what so-called "Red Flag" laws are all about. But ideally, he notes, if someone with anger issues has a gun, a concerned citizen, friend or neighbor would reach out and try to help that person with their issues and keep them from hurting someone and going to prison.

Some would caution against getting involved with other people's business at all, for a variety of reasons that Moe understands—the primary one being trust, or lack thereof. "I think the relationship between police and community is so far off now that they got a lot of work to do to even make people want to practice citizenship in these communities where they don't trust the police. Everything depends on trust. A citizen has got to be able to trust that if they call the police, the police are not going to come and just beat the fuck out of a person because they got a gun, or because they are doing something wrong. If you can't trust that they're going to do that right, then you're not going to call the police."

It's complicated, Moe says, expressing a preference for more accountability in the community, better communication, and building trust with the police. "The police work for us, we don't work for the police. That's one of the mistakes that people make. And I understand that this system of law enforcement has never been right to us, going back to slavery. So that's embedded in us. But at some point, we got to fix it."

The Real Meaning of "Snitching"

Washington Post, August 19, 2007

By Ronald Moten

A hundred people gathered at Washington's Scripture Cathedral in May, many of them teenagers from the surrounding O Street NW neighborhood, where a murderous street feud had terrorized the community. Our anti-violence group, Peaceoholics, had convened a forum to ask, "What's Snitching and What's Not?"

Snitching—and its sibling, witness intimidation—is much in the news these days, the result of a series of high-profile killings and shootings both here in the Washington area and elsewhere. But there are a lot of myths and misconceptions about it, not just among people in the community, but also among law enforcement officials and the media.

Trying to break the ice at our forum, I threw out a few questions: If someone shot your mother during a drive-by, would you have a problem with that? Would you want something to happen to that person? Would it make more sense for you to be locked up, or would you like the shooter to be incarcerated?

There wasn't much of a response until a young man came forward. "I ain't no snitch," he said. "But I'll help the community."

Nobody wants to be a snitch—not even in a forum that's supposed to define what exactly snitching is.

My job is to try to bring peace to the community. But I'm also realistic: You are never going to get black people to agree to snitch. The reasons are rooted in history and culture, and the realities of so many inner cities, where human life is cheap.

But as someone who has been on the other side of the law, what I will say is that if you work at it, you can persuade witnesses to violent crime to come forward.

For those of us who live in high-crime areas, there's nothing new about witness intimidation—criminals threatening or even killing citizens who could testify against them. But several recent incidents have brought wider attention to this issue.

In Newark, witnesses have fingered the suspects in 14 recent killings, but prosecutors have not charged them for fear that the witnesses who identified them would be hurt or killed. Rap artists and gang leaders in Baltimore and Boston have recently begun campaigns urging city residents to "Stop Snitching." The rapper Cam'ron was interviewed on "60 Minutes" about why he refused to cooperate with police after he was shot in the arm in Washington during a botched carjacking in 2005.

And last week, Prince George's County prosecutors blamed witness intimidation for their failure to win convictions in two homicide cases. In the fall of 2005, Lakita Danielle Tolson, a 19-year-old mother and nursing student, was killed outside a Temple Hills nightclub. Nine months later, Eric S. Holland, 18, was killed in a crowded schoolyard. Law enforcement and family members believe he was targeted because people (wrongly) thought he was cooperating with police on the Tolson case. Large crowds were at both shootings, but only one witness agreed to testify in both cases.

I've told the young people at our snitching forums that if they see someone killed, it's their obligation to help make sure that the killer is punished. The government works for us, and together we can hold it to higher standards.

But words and connotations are powerful. And to many of us, the word "snitch" brings to mind a distant memory of a house slave telling the master when another slave tried to escape. We're a long way from the days of slavery, but the adversity that those of us trapped in communities with little money, education and police protection share has forced us to create our own codes and coping strategies.

So often, even law-abiding residents try to close ranks and deal with our problems on our own instead of working with law enforcement, which many of us consider the enemy. It's a code, just like the one some think Scooter Libby upheld at the White House, or the one police adhere to when they cover up for crooked cops.

As someone who was once part of the problem, I have some insight into this issue. I grew up in the Petworth neighborhood in the 1970s and '80s. Before I turned my life around, I was incarcerated several times for selling drugs. I believe that jail saved me.

Once, during those days, I was accused of being a snitch. In 1990, I found myself at the apartment of an older associate who'd been set up by some Colombians. The police raided the place, found drugs and locked us both up. I posted bail and was released on bond. The old head wasn't. When I got out on the street, rumors flew that I had told on him and that's why I'd been freed. It wasn't until the guy was released and set the record straight that my name was cleared. I did not and would not snitch—not then, not now.

This is the true definition of a snitch: someone who commits a crime but then blames an accomplice so that he can negotiate a lighter sentence or even go free. Often he tells lies and incriminates the innocent. People like that are the real snitches and they are cowardly. Snitching is a way for criminals to game the system.

But not everyone who talks to police is a snitch. If you're a victim of a crime and you or someone you trust cooperates with them, you are not a snitch. If you try to get rid of negativity in your community, you are not "hot" or a snitch.

I blame the hip-hop industry for spreading confusion about the definition of snitching. I also understand that the artists are just trying to sell records by glorifying a criminal and prison culture they often know nothing about.

At the O Street forum, I broke it down for the young people: Say that a group of dudes are serving time peacefully, with workout and other privileges. If some knucklehead comes into the unit to mess up their peace by violating prison rules, what do they do?

"Kill them," the audience replied.

No, I told them. They drop a note—some might say snitch—to get that person out of their unit. I'm not saying it's right or wrong, but most people who have never been locked up don't understand this. You do what you have to do to keep your own peace.

Understanding snitching is not just a theoretical exercise. It is critical to the survival of our communities. As I was writing this, I received a call from a woman who lives in a District housing project. She was active with youth and outspoken about crime in her neighborhood. Thugs broke into her apartment and shot her son, a college student, in the legs. Where is the discussion about this in the community? Why is this behavior allowed to continue?

Just as we have a right to be safe from drive-by shootings, murder, intimidation and disrespect, we have an obligation to uphold the laws that ensure public safety. When a citizen witnesses a crime and decides to be civically responsible, this doesn't constitute snitching; it's doing the right thing.

Police also need to be more sensitive to the culture of the streets. Showing up in uniform and knocking on someone's door could get an innocent person killed. If police are clumsy in their investigations and let word out about who is cooperating, that can also lead to more bloodshed, something Eric Holland learned the hard way.

The Peaceoholics plan to conduct many more forums, not only on snitching, but also on what it means to be a responsible citizen. In previous forums we asked participants to answer several questions in an anonymous survey. "If someone killed my brother or sister I would [fill in the blank]."

Among the responses: "Kill them." "Cooperate." "Retaliate." "Go tell the police." And something that I have seen all too often: "Already happened. I would go look for them and talk to them face to face and ask them why."

People in the community want peace, and they want justice. They just don't want to be anybody's snitch.

Chapter 14

"High" Crimes and Misdemeanors

It never ceases to amaze me how Moe's words resonate so many years after he's written them. Almost a decade after this 2012 piece for the *Washington Times* on decriminalizing marijuana, the issues are still ripe for discussion, even as society is headed for widespread legalization.

He recalls a community meeting at the Anacostia Library at the time, and that he didn't like what he was hearing. "I felt like this legislation was being pushed down our throats, and it wasn't vetted, and people weren't thinking that out," Moe says, down in the basement of Check It Enterprises about a week before Thanksgiving 2019. "And while I do agree that African Americans were victims of disparities with the marijuana laws, what I was looking at was two things: One, there has to be an education piece before you do something as drastic as this because of what I saw with our young people in our community. And two, an employment piece, because a lot of young people who were in Career Connections, Project Empowerment, and other programs, they can't be in them if they had dirty urine."

> What I'm saying is, you don't rush policy. You think out the pros and cons and you do it right. And this wasn't done right.

Actually, Moe has more than two objections. He's also concerned about the effects of marijuana on young brains and bodies that are still developing, particularly given the potency of marijuana these days: "I've talked to several principals in D.C. public schools, and they said at least half their children come to school high," he says, adding that the extra cost of high-grade, mood-altering weed lures kids into stealing, robbing, and drug dealing so they can afford it. These things were not part of the discussion when legalization advocates were lobbying the D.C. Council, he points out. "Well, I know the guy, Adam Eidinger, he was, you know, out here hustling. And it was a lot of money poured into it from sources outside of our community, by people who don't care about what happens inside of it."

Moe recalls going to meet Eidinger and his partner with a fellow community activist, Ivan Cloyd. "We went and just simply asked one thing: 'Could you include education for our young people about marijuana into your whole movement and, if you do that, I really won't have a problem with it.' And they refused. They were like, 'That's not our mission.' And that seems to me to say a lot."

At the time of this op-ed, medical marijuana was still a hot topic. Moe was having discussions with then–Ward 7 Councilmember Yvette Alexander, who wanted to include migraines, digestive ailments, and post-traumatic stress disorder to the list of conditions for which one could get a prescription. Moe says Alexander was against decriminalization, which seems inconsistent. "Well, my thing was if marijuana helps with any ailment that anybody has, I'm with it. I think marijuana can be a great drug. Like I'll give you a prime example: I've used CBD rubs for pain I had in my shoulder, and it worked. So I'm not saying that the plant doesn't have benefits. What I'm saying is, you don't rush policy. You think out the pros and cons and you do it right. And this wasn't done right."

Ironically, Alexander is now a lobbyist in the healthcare industry with business interests in legalized marijuana, which has become very lucrative. Moe hopes that having been in public service, Alexander maintains a balance that's in the best interests of those most affected by the policies she is advocating.

Meanwhile, today D.C. smells like weed wherever you go. For Moe, this presents another problem: It's legal to possess, but smoking in public—or even possessing it on federal property, or in public housing complexes—is illegal. "Well, with the marijuana decriminalization, from my understanding, more people were locked up for marijuana after this law passed than before, for smoking it in the streets," he says. "But once again, there was no education component, and most people didn't know what they could and couldn't do. Many people still end up getting records, which is directly going against what you say you were doing this for. So it had an adverse effect even from that perspective."

Another consequence of decriminalization is that a black market for marijuana has thrived, which can ensnare those who are not eligible to get into the legitimate flow of commerce. This is where Moe's experience as a returned citizen shapes his views: "I just think if you're going to legalize it, everybody should have a shot at making money," he says. "I say give [returned citizens] a shot if that's how y'all want to do it. For real. It shouldn't be a monopoly on it. I feel like that has forced people who were on the streets to get into the black market. Then they gotta sneak around and do it instead of making it legal for them to do it. Make it a process and make them a part of it. This could be a first and a second chance for many in my community."

Regardless of policy distinctions, the money in weed is so big these days that it has attracted more violent crime than ever, Moe says. "That can have something to do with crime going up. You have popups, people get shot at the popups, robbed at popups."

Even as we speak, the D.C. Council is debating whether to crack down on the practice of "gifting" marijuana to customers who buy merchandise such as a t-shirt or a hat, or other consumables such as juice or baked goods. (No pun intended.)

The marijuana movement also has resulted in changes in Moe's community and in his social circle, now that pot is no longer illegal: "Oh, there's no question about it. I mean, it's a popular high, man. Probably half of my friends use marijuana. What I'm concerned about, all of 'em are smoking all day, every day. You know, it went from an occasional thing to an everyday thing, two or three times a day."

That doesn't bode well for getting or keeping a job, Moe believes, pointing to the downsides of excessive use that he has seen take a toll on people he knows—even intelligent and successful ones, he says. "If you knew that was going to be a problem, you should have probably worked on that before you passed the legislation. You know, in a city where African Americans have a hard time gaining employment, why would you add more barriers to the population, when institutionalized racism and disparities are embedded in our laws, breeding all the chaos we see in society today?"

The Political and Moral Contradictions of Decriminalizing Marijuana

Washington Times, October 24, 2012

By Ron Moten

Last night at the Anacostia town hall meeting on the decriminalization of marijuana, issues were raised on both sides of the controversy. These are the same issues that face District of Columbia City Council members as they prepare for an upcoming vote on Councilmember Tommy Wells' bill that would decriminalize marijuana. For the proponents of legalization, this is the next logical step now that lobbyists for medical marijuana have won their battle, but it has also resulted in many political and moral contradictions and conflicts.

One of the justifications for decriminalization is a recent study by the ACLU which concludes that Blacks and Whites use the drug at about the same rate even though 9 out of 10 people locked up for marijuana in D.C. are Black or other minorities. Others, like Lydell Mann who uses what he calls an herb, not a drug, asked preachers, "Which one of you were there to hear God tell Adam and Eve what herbs to use and not to use?" Mann said marijuana helped him recover from pain and serious injury. He argues that full legalization is warranted based on research that demonstrates marijuana's many health benefits. Others make the argument that marijuana use also has negative effects such as increased cases of asthma, financial distress and, especially in poor neighborhoods, habitual self-medication and often a gateway to other narcotics.

Ward 7 Councilmember Yvette Alexander opposes Wells' bill. She was quoted in the City Paper by Will Sommer as saying, "I say if it's illegal, keep it illegal." She has a valid point given that Ward 7 has many children who often arrive late to school smelling like a pound of weed. She also has employers complaining that her constituents are not employable because they can't come with clean urine. But then Alexander contradicted herself when she learned that there are so few D.C. residents taking advantage of the opportunity to have marijuana legally prescribed by a doctor for medical reasons.

Alexander suddenly became concerned with the fact that the marijuana dispensaries are losing money rather than becoming cash cows for the D.C. treasury as expected. Once that came to her attention, she hinted that she was open to expanding the list of diseases approved for its use beyond those already included such as HIV/AIDS and cancer. Now she wants to include migraine headaches, digestive ailments and post-traumatic stress disorder. If she is against its decriminalization, why expand its availability for medicinal purposes simply because there are not enough people using this miracle drug?

It's interesting, but not surprising how quickly politicians abandon strongly stated moral positions when money becomes the issue. The so-called "war on drugs" has always been about money, not about what is right or wrong. (For documentation on the history of how both Democratic and Republican law makers, judges and law enforcement agencies benefit from the mass incarceration of Black men resulting from the war on drugs, read the book by Michelle Alexander The New Jim Crow.) Now many liberal politicians are figuring out how to generate more revenue for the government through the decriminalization of marijuana. It starts with medical use and decriminalization, but once that genie is out of the bottle, harder drugs will follow.

Mayor Vincent Gray knows how to spin the issue so he cannot be accused of legalizing marijuana. Just like with traffic cameras, Gray made it clear that for him it is all about the money, not about morals or safety when he said, "Having marijuana shouldn't mean jail, but not paying your bill should." The idea is to create a new revenue stream for the District by reducing the possession of small amounts of marijuana to a civil offense and fining offenders $100. While current penalties under federal law for possession of marijuana are certainly too harsh and destructive to people of color, Wells and his supporters are, at the very least, ignoring the arguments that contradict their own stated concerns about our children's education and soaring Black unemployment.

Reducing possession to a civil offense will dramatically affect both school and job performance. Decriminalization in D.C. does not mean employers won't drug test employees. Are the mayor, the council and their progressive pot-smoking supporters ready to fund assistance for those who lose their jobs or drop out of school because their drug of choice will be so easily accessible and the penalty for possession so light? Will there be mandatory drug addiction and education classes for those who go from recreational use to self-medication? What about adults like Maryland Democratic gubernatorial candidate Douglas Gansler who make lame excuses for not stopping underage drinking? Why should we think it will be different with marijuana?

While the District might decriminalize marijuana, employers, including the city's largest, the federal government, still have drug testing. Isn't it hard enough for Blacks to get jobs with a real unemployment rate of 25 percent overall and 50 percent for Black teens without making such a popular drug even more accessible? Who is going to hire someone with dirty urine for a construction job driving heavy equipment or for a position in a federal agency that requires a security clearance? The argument that alcohol abuse is the same as drug use is not true. Alcohol leaves the system in hours, marijuana takes 30 days. Wells, the general leading the battle for this "legislation of goodwill" acknowledged this himself when he admitted that it will be difficult to get employers to relax their drug policies since that would make it harder for them to get insurance.

Doing what is socially popular and generates more money for the government might not be the right thing to do for our most vulnerable citizens. Our leaders need to face their own political and moral contradictions on this issue and then come up with legislation that helps fix our broken criminal justice system rather than passing a law that could cause more problems.

Chapter 15

Humane Treatment in Prison Would Enhance Reentry into Society

The invasion of the U.S. Capitol on January 6, 2021, was something most Americans, and especially most Washingtonians, likely never envisioned, and the images from that day remain surreal: the thousands of insurrectionists climbing walls and scaffolding to breach the building; the teargas and the bear spray; the violence and destruction; the pure rage.

More than a year later, the U.S. Attorney for the District of Columbia is still prosecuting and convicting Proud Boys, Oath Keepers, and their fellow travelers, and federal judges are handing down sentences that range from five months to five years. Dozens of these defendants have spent time at a terrible place that far too many Black District residents know all too well: D.C. Jail.

So it was infuriating to Moe, and to those who have served or worked with returning citizens, when aggrieved White men and women were able to attract national media attention with their complaints about abusive guards, disgusting food, seeping sewage, and vermin at the jail. "Tell us something we don't know" was the reaction from inmates, their families, and advocates, who have protested these and other inhumane conditions in the face of institutional indifference for decades.

> "It's up to people in the community to step up, but it's also up to government to do better," says Moe. "And I think we can do better. That's why me and Big G did what we did.

In fact, just nine months earlier, Moe and Anwan "Big G" Glover (of Backyard Band and The Wire) co-authored this piece for the Washington *Post*, protesting unsanitary conditions at the jail as Covid-19 was coursing through the inmate population. "We were getting all these calls from the jail, me and G—people blowing our phones up and getting family members to call us," Moe says of the outrage his community felt, in the early days of the pandemic. "I felt compelled to do something because I was in D.C. Jail in 1991, and it hasn't changed too much since then."

They organized a "sleep out" for the following night, with fellow activists camping outside the jail in sleeping bags and tents, while inside, prisoners were expressing their appreciation: "I'll never forget that day, when guys was banging on the windows when we were out there, and it felt good to know that people appreciate you and that we were there fighting for the people that people often forget about."

[*Photo: Weensy, Anwan "Big G" Glover, and Moe at D.C. Jail sleep-out to advocate for better conditions.*]

They didn't want it to be overtly political, Moe says; they wanted to show support for edible food, cleaner conditions, and for more programs for inmates who, someday, will be re-entering society. "We didn't blast it out to a million people because we didn't want that type of environment. We just wanted people we knew who really cared, not to do photo ops and leave. We wanted people to stay there all night. And it was powerful."

Moe was arrested in 1991 and charged with felony drug trafficking. His incarceration began at D.C. Jail, where the majority of inmates are awaiting adjudication or serving time for misdemeanor offenses. In 1992, at age 21, he was convicted and sentenced to federal prison. He went on to serve four years, first at a facility in Danbury, Connecticut, where he earned his high school diploma, and then in Allenwood, Pennsylvania, where he enrolled in community college.

Having experienced the good and the bad of the prison system, he says, the bottom line is that the District needs a new jail, one that is clean, safe, and tailored for true rehabilitation, and large enough to house the local incarcerated population. But because of D.C. Jail's size, as well as its jurisdictional limitations—and the closure in the late 1990s of the infamous Lorton Reformatory—those facing lengthier sentences are scattered across the country, leaving them isolated, unable to see family and friends who can give them hope and remind them that there's something to come home to:

"D.C. prisoners are being shipped to prisons around the country because we don't have our own facility. We have family members calling about how they're being treated in private prisons. If you treat people inhumanely when they're locked up, you can't expect them to come home and be good people." (In March, as this book was nearing completion, Mayor Bowser issued a budget proposal that includes $250 million over six-years for an annex to the correctional treatment facility at the jail, and $25 million to "maintain safe, secure, and humane conditions" at the main detention facility. Construction of the annex, however, won't begin until 2026, as the bulk of the funding is budgeted for fiscal years 2027 and 2028.)

One of the subjects Moe and I have often discussed over the years is the importance of community. Indeed, it is a central theme of this book. And as much as some semblance of community—and humanity—is crucial to rehabilitation in both prison and youth correctional facilities, it becomes even more essential when ex-offenders return home.

"Well, 'The Village' is everything," says Moe, whose grandparents and groundbreaking pastor and civil rights lawyer Dovey Roundtree supported and advocated for him when he was incarcerated. Then a more recent encounter came to mind: "I was at Hope Village halfway house. We were outside, and this guy came home from federal prison after 42 years. It was like 10 at night. He had a bus ticket, and he was like, 'I had to find my way here. I don't have no children. I don't have a mother or father. I don't have nobody alive.' That's what he came home to, because we don't have our own facilities here where we can do a real re-entry program and connect our citizens to the people and programs in a community. It's hard to prepare for that from 300 miles away."

Moe points to the work of the Mayor's Office on Returning Citizens Affairs, which has established a model that can make a difference in the lives of those who don't want to repeat past mistakes, but who also don't have much to fall back on: "There was small things they did, like you come home, you get a driver's license, birth certificate—which are hard for somebody who just came home. And they made it easy to help people with child support, traffic tickets, and things that often stagnate people in the process of going back home."

Sensationalized media coverage of D.C. Jail's conditions following the January 6 arrests shortchanged the pain of the persistent conditions local offenders suffer year after year, Moe says, as we sat in the Secret Garden out back of the Check It Enterprises storefront on a cold day in March, a little more than a year after the Capitol insurrection. It was an unwelcome reminder of how the press applies a double standard for Black and White inmates, he says. "It was like when those [rioters] came to the jail their issues were more valid than the issues our people have had. Like there's no empathy for the people from D.C. we talk about all the time."

Empathy starts at home, however. "It's up to people in the community to step up, but it's also up to the government to do better," says Moe. "And I think we can do better. That's why me and Big G did what we did. We didn't do it to point fingers, we did it to say: 'Listen, we still got to fix this. This is a broken record that we can fix, that we need to fix.'"

D.C. Should Act Now to Save the Lives
of Returning Citizens

Washington Post, April 27, 2020

By Ron Moten and Anwan "Big G" Glover

Ralph Anwan "Big G" Glover is an actor, philanthropist and leader of the Backyard Band. Ronald "Moe" Moten is the co-founder of Check It Enterprises and Don't Mute DC.

Over the past few weeks, our phones have been ringing off the hook with desperate calls from the families of our incarcerated friends in the D.C. Jail and Hope Village. No toilet paper. No running water. No cleaning supplies.

These calls have escalated from fear to horror as they have watched 81 of their fellow inmates become infected and at least one die from the novel coronavirus. Covid-19, the disease that develops from the coronavirus, is racing through D.C. jails at 15 times the rate of the general population, according to the Justice Policy Institute.

These voices haunt us. They are insistent. We can't sleep. We have no choice but to amplify their pain and suffering outside the walls that conceal them. So, we have decided to take action. On Tuesday night, we have assembled a few good men and women as part of the new organization called "70K Strong." We are bringing our sleeping bags and tents for a "social distancing" sleep-out outside the D.C. Jail. We hope that you listen to what we and our partners have to say.

We write to you as returned citizens and men of conscience. Our brothers and sisters are rotting in unsanitary conditions in the D.C. Jail, the Hope Village reentry facility and the 102 prisons around the country, many of them for-profit.

Without urgent action, they will face certain death from the coronavirus. Without structural changes in the way we address mass incarceration and the District's role in it, they will be abandoned to a liminal space between life and death. This is a hell that no human being deserves.

Unfortunately, we know firsthand how horrible jail conditions are. Before one of us, Big G, became leader of Backyard Band and an actor and philanthropist known for his iconic role of Slim Charles in HBO's "The Wire," he was sent to juvenile detention in Texas as an 11-year-old. Before the other of us, Moe, became the community activist known for organizing the Unity Clothing association of D.C. designers, Don't Mute DC and the Go-Go Museum & Cafe, he spent time in D.C. Jail and in Lorton in the early 1990s.

Like Chuck Brown, who learned to play the guitar in Lorton Correctional Facility and later created go-go, the city's official music, we paid our debts to society and went on to contribute to our city. In the mid-1990s, when we were both working with the peace organization Cease Fire Don't Smoke the Brothers and Sisters, we laid in the streets to protest budget cuts that took music and trades out of D.C. public schools.

Today, we are facing the biggest moral crisis we have seen in our lives.

Unfortunately, this crisis did not begin with the coronavirus. The federal government controls our criminal justice system. It closed the Lorton correctional facility and sent incarcerated people to prisons across the country. Because of that, most Washingtonians who do a local crime serve time in federal prisons dispersed across the United States.

Right now, D.C. residents are serving time in 102 federal and for-profit prisons across the United States. An epidemiological model recently released by the American Civil Liberties Union and academic researchers predict that an additional 100,000 people will die in prison from covid-19 if we don't reduce the prison population.

On Feb. 18, 2019, the D.C. auditor released a damning report stating conditions inside the D.C. Jail are hazardous to inmates and staff. The report discussed mold growing on walls, faulty shower stalls and inhumane temperatures.

Today, the District is in a much better financial place than it was in the 1990s, even with the unfortunate revenue reductions because of the coronavirus pandemic. We see cranes reaching the sky in every direction for upscale commercial, retail and housing developments. The city can invest in making conditions for D.C.'s incarcerated more humane. The District can build safe and effective jails and reentry facilities and bring our people home. To do otherwise means potentially adding covid-19 to their sentence. Our elected officials did not create mass incarceration or the conditions that allowed so much of our human capital to be locked behind bars. But the mayor and D.C. Council can address this calamity. We ask that they:

- Expedite improving D.C. Jail conditions, starting with installing a new heating and cooling system, providing sanitary supplies and building a new jail immediately.

- Work with the Bureau of Prisons to expedite opening new reentry center immediately as Hope Village is slated to close on April 30.

- Release D.C. residents who are federally sentenced and who have good behavior and are serving time in the 102 jails around the country.

- Regain control of parole from the Federal Bureau of Prisons. These life-or-death decisions about who gets parole should not be made by people with no connection to our community.

Taking control of our criminal system is a critical step toward true self-determination and statehood.

Chapter 16

What a Crane Will Never Lift

Washington Post, May 4, 2014

By Ron Moten

The painful days of regularly seeing yellow tape and hearing police sirens was, to some degree, becoming a thing of the past in the District. The chief of police was praised universally, and our politicians frequently pointed to the reduction in homicides and other crimes in speeches. The city has been flooded with those new Washingtonians that our leaders sought for so long.

That was yesterday. What about today? I can't help but worry whether things are moving backward. The murder rate is up 75 percent compared with this time last year. The city has averaged nine murders a month over the past four months. Many of them occurred in broad daylight.

This is especially discouraging for those of us who helped the last administration draft and implement an effective plan called the Focus Improvement Area Initiative. It empowered concerned individuals and organizations to work on behalf of the community to broker truces between rival gangs in areas prone to homicides and violence, such as Anacostia and Columbia Heights. This was a genuine partnership among community leaders, organizations and government agencies that brought about healing for families and empowered people from within those communities to solve their own problems. We knew where the problems were; collectively we attacked them. It was exactly what was needed. The benefits were dramatic.

The root causes of crime are complex, but it is simple enough for those of us who have been in the trenches to make an assessment and come up with accurate and honest conclusions. Five years ago, city leaders understood the concept that "hurt people hurt people" taught to us by icons of the civil rights movement. Once you embrace the wisdom of that saying, you also understand that "healed people heal people." I know this from personal experience as a young person who hurt my community through crime and then, after being healed, returned to help my community.

Somehow, though, the city has drifted away from solutions that were empowering people to reduce violence and bring healing to our communities. Now, politicians point to the number of cranes over the District as a measure of good government, not to the health and safety of its citizens. Economic development is important, but no number of cranes can make up for the price we pay if we fail to address issues of the heart. That kind of math throws our moral, spiritual and social compasses out of whack. It relegates all our hurt people with damaged hearts to lives of fear and grief rather than empowering them from within to heal themselves and others.

Affordable housing is disappearing. Homelessness has reached crisis levels. Our public schools continue to fail far too many of our children. A rising tide doesn't lift all boats. It swamps a lot of them.

On Easter Monday, I was worried when I went down to the National Zoo. When the annual event started in the 19th century as an alternative for black families who could not attend the Whites-only White House Easter Egg Roll, it was a wonderful family celebration. In those days, African Americans had a proud tradition of intact families. Today, the data are astonishing: Only 9 percent of black 15- to 17-year-olds in the city live in households with a married mother and father.

When I was a teenager, Easter Monday was a family day. Not anymore. The few families I saw this year came early, but that gave way to crews of kids roaming about on their own. Then, despite the countless police and other officials I saw, what I prayed would not happen happened. I heard gunshots at the zoo. Two teenagers were shot.

We need to make our families whole again. We need to address the issues of the heart. Maybe the recent increase in murders is just a blip, but if it's not, it won't be a crane that lifts us off this downward path. It will be the arms of the community, one person at a time.

Artwork: Michaye McIlwain

Epilogue

Moe and I were out back behind Check It Enterprises' Martin Luther King Avenue headquarters in Bundy's Secret Garden last March, thinking about all we had set out to do with this collection of his writings, and how they all fit together.

"The Secret Garden" is named for Alexander "Bundy" Mosby, who along with Check It's other neighbors led a group of volunteers that rolled up their sleeves and cleaned out what had become a nuisance, infested with rats and vermin, so the space could be put to good use. Bundy had owned the clothing store District Culture at 1922 MLK Ave. and was planning to open an upscale lounge there, until he was among 13 people killed over a deadly Memorial Day weekend in 2018.

The Secret Garden is the heart of Check It's universe, the spiritual center. Hovering above its stage are murals of D.C. icons Congresswoman Eleanor Holmes Norton, legendary activist-turned-media personality Petey Greene, Marion Barry with a raised fist, and the Frederick Douglass House. Throughout much of the pandemic, this stage has continued to serve as a venue for Go-Go performances, vigils, and community gatherings, so it felt right to come back to this place where we had been meeting since 2019 to talk about the wealth of civil rights history and urban wisdom contained in this book.

> Are we going to invest in our own community and develop our own community? Or are we going to follow our colonizers?

It also felt appropriate in that Check It recently landed the property rights to the Secret Garden from developer Douglas Jemal, who, as it turned out, held title to the once-abandoned lot and had threatened to evict the group—or, at best, only lease rather than sell it to Check It.

This was no small problem. With the help of a $2 million city grant, Check It already owned its storefront and the two adjacent ones on either side: We Act Radio's studio and a creative art and food space that fellow entrepreneur and socialite Darnell Perkins plans to open in the near future. They also were eyeing a purchase of a fourth adjacent property someday. With the Go-Go Museum expected to open at Check It in the coming months, Moe and his partners are primed to launch what they hope will become the Black cultural hub of the entire East Coast. Having to lease the Secret Garden would have been unacceptable—not for an enterprise built to be a model of ownership and self-determination.

But instead of "going to war" with Jemal, Moe persuaded the notoriously brash and stubborn developer that selling the parcel to activists who had rescued the trash-strewn lot and created a thriving multi-use site—host to a vegetable garden, bee colony, and many fish frys—was the right thing to do.

There was some symbolism to the day as well. As we sat out back, talking about Moe's journey from returned citizen to activist, to community advocate, to youth mentor, to historian of the civil rights movement, to entrepreneur and museum curator, a multistory brick building was under construction right next door, with its looming cranes. We laughed at the stark contrast, and about how the Secret Garden exists despite the cookie-cutter development at the dark heart of gentrification. We were struck how this book's final op-ed, published in the *Washington Post* in 2014, encapsulates his whole journey, and his philosophy and his vision of creating positive change measured, not by more cranes, but by "addressing the issues of the heart ... one person at a time."

It was hard to sit there on the deck, in the shadows of yet another one of the typical, boxy multi-use buildings you see all over town and not think: This development boom in Anacostia is just getting started. But for whose benefit? So much of what has gone into this book speaks to the struggle of D.C.'s Black community to attain its fair share of the city's good fortunes. Gentrification, as we have known it, is still a White man's game, which is not to deny that plenty of Black businessmen and women with the right connections are getting in on, and often directing, the action.

Like Moe often says, "gentrification" is a word that could be redefined as a positive process if it was more equitable and tailored to improving communities for the benefit of the people who live there. For instance, Black businesses are making unprecedented inroads in Ward 8, he says, running down a list of Black-owned development companies engaged in nearby projects, and then pointing out: residents also want a chance to be a part of and profit from the gentrification that is coming to their community. Take a stroll past the Big Chair in downtown Anacostia, head up to Congress Heights to the Sports Arena and St. Elizabeth's East Campus, and you're gonna see, it's already happening, he adds.

It occurred to me that when you take an organic view, it makes sense that Moe's approach to building people up so they can take control of their own lives and futures is a virtual metaphor for the rehabilitation and redevelopment of fallow and blighted properties scattered across our city. The difference, according to him, is that erecting shiny new buildings is not the answer for healing and lifting up damaged lives. "This shit is spiritual," he says of the teachings and mentorship that he believes is giving disadvantaged youth from all sorts of backgrounds the tools to rise up and realize their own dreams. "You got to look 'em in the eye, so they can feel your soul. If you don't believe you can change their mindset, then you should quit. If you don't think you can knock out Muhammad Ali, you ain't gonna knock out Ali. He's gonna smell fear."

Once again, this op-ed shows that Moe's words resonate today, just as much as they did when he wrote them more than seven years ago. As I looked over at the murals behind the stage, and then up at the soulless construction rising up above us at the other end of the Secret Garden, I realized that this piece really does sum up the vision of this urban scholar.

Moe was feeling it too, I sensed, as he snatched up a copy of his op-ed off the table between the two of us and began shaking the pages in his hand.

"How can we be here, eight years later, and the same model of growth and development still threatens underserved communities by enriching the privileged, while leaving the people behind?" he asked, voice raised, energized by the weight of his own words. "Are we gonna invest in our own community and develop our own community? Or are we gonna follow our colonizers?"

The answers, Moe would argue, will not come by remaining silent.

Photos

Moe's decades of tireless determination to speak for his people has earned him a place at the table with local and national politicians, civil rights pioneers, and community leaders.

Arrington Dixon, Moe, and "Mayor for Life" Marion Barry

Moe advocating at one of many D.C. Council hearings

Sen. Tim Scott and Attorney General Karl Racine attend one of Moe's focus groups in the Check It Enterprises community room

Martin Luther King III, Moe, and Dick Gregory
talk to media after Moe's annual MLK event
honoring community heroes

Ed, Sen. Tim Scott, Rep. Eleanor Holmes Norton,
and Moe at the Secret Garden

Stevie Wonder and Moe. Stevie accepted Moe's invitation
to perform at Ballou High School PTA meeting
in support of parents and teachers.

Former Mayor Adrian Fenty joins Moe at Peaceoholics
peace rally at Freedom Plaza in Washington, D.C.

Moe calls press conference with plan to address violence
in SE D.C. joined by former Mayors Adrian Fenty and Marion Barry

The Don't Mute DC Movement organized a rally at United Medical Center which helped persuade elected officials to put $25 million into D.C.'s only hospital east of the river. It serves over 160,000 citizens, many who live in poverty. This will keep the hospital operating until the new hospital opens in 2024.

Don't Mute DC rally at United Medical Center

Go-Go bands play at Don't Mute DC UMC rally

Nurses speak at Don't Mute DC United Medical Center rally

Roc Mickey, Moe, and Tony Lewis, Jr. at UMC rally

Moe speaking at Don't Mute DC press conference announcing victory against gentrifiers as the music returned to the Don Campbell's Metro PCS Store in the gentrified Shaw community.

Don Campbell, the courageous owner of the Metro PCS store called Moe for help and the rest was history.

Moe testifies at D.C. Council hearing to make Go-Go the official music of the District of Columbia

Moe and Sugar Bear from EU with Mayor Bowser at signing to make Go-Go the official music of the District of Columbia

Promo lit for sleep-out at D.C. Jail
organized by Moe and "Big G"

Moe, Erica Briscoe, Starr Bennett at
D.C. Jail sleep-out

Howard University student Julien Broomfield created #DontMuteDC.

Moe and Howard University professor Dr. Natalie Hopkinson, co-founder of Don't Mute DC

Anwan "Big G" Glover and Backyard Band on Don't Mute DC
Go-Go float on Juneteenth near where the movement started

Photo credit: Samuel Johnson, photographer

Thousands of youths marching with Moe and Anwan
"Big G" Glover in 2008 during the Peaceoholics
annual Atonement March

Moe, Tony Lewis, Jr., and Eric Weaver advocating for Returned Citizens at a D.C. Council hearing.

Anwan "Big G" Glover (c) and Moe leading protest advocating for returning citizens

H Street Halfway House Rally

Thousands of D.C. Returning Citizens did not have a halfway house to come home to. Moe and Don't Mute DC helped organize the people to help advocates push aside the roadblocks stopping a new halfway house from opening in D.C. The halfway house is now under construction.

TCB Band plays at Don't Mute DC Halfway house rally in Chinatown, Washington, D.C

Youth dance at halfway house rally on New York Ave.

Moe with Bo from TCB Band

Chinatown halfway house rally

Thousands attend halfway house rally on New York Ave

Above and Below: New York Ave halfway house rally

Moe with supporters at halfway house rally

Weensy from Backyard Band
performing at rally

Moe speaking at rally before Sugar
Bear and E.U. performance.

Illustration by Xueying Chang, Ralph Rinzler
Folklife Archives, Smithsonian Institution.